EXCELL___

SHORT
WALKS
IN THE NORTH ISLAND

EXCELLENT SHORT WALKS

IN THE NORTH ISLAND

250 WALKS UNDER 2 HOURS

PETER JANSSEN

NH
NEW HOLLAND

To Phil and Gary, for being the best of friends.

First published in 2007 by New Holland Publishers (NZ) Ltd
Auckland • Sydney • London • Cape Town

218 Lake Road, Northcote, Auckland 0627, New Zealand
Unit 1, 66 Gibbes Street, Chatswood, NSW 2067, Australia
86–88 Edgware Road, London W2 2EA, United Kingdom
Wembley Square, First floor, Solan Road, Gardens, Cape Town 8001, South Africa

www.newhollandpublishers.co.nz

Copyright © 2007 in text: Peter Janssen
Copyright © 2007 in photography: Peter Janssen, except where otherwise credited
Copyright © 2007 New Holland Publishers (NZ) Ltd

Publishing Manager: Christine Thomson
Editor: Alison Southby
Design team: Graeme Leather/IslandBridge, Dee Murch
Cover photograph: Shaun Barnett/Black Robin Photography
Cover design: Trevor Newman
Maps: Bruce McLennan/IslandBridge

National Library of New Zealand Cataloguing-in-Publication Data

Janssen, Peter (Peter Leon)
Excellent short walks in the North Island : 250 walks under 2
hours / Peter Janssen, author and photographer ; Alison
Southby, editor.
(Excellent short walks)
ISBN 978-1-86966-172-4
1. Trails—New Zealand—North Island. 2. North Island (N.Z.)—
Description and travel. I. Southby, Alison. II. Title. III. Series.
796.5109931—dc 22

Colour reproduction by Pica Digital Pte Ltd, Singapore
Printed by Times Offset (M) Sdn Bhd, Malaysia, on paper that has been sourced from sustainable forests

10 9 8 7 6 5 4

Contents

Introduction   13

Acknowledgements   16

Northland   17

  1   Cape Reinga   18
  2   Te Paki Sand Hills   19
  3   St Paul's Rock, Whangaroa Harbour   19
  4   Puketi Kauri Forest   20
  5   Kerikeri Basin   20
  6   Mangroves, Waitangi   22
  7   Paihia Lookout   22
  8   Urupukapuka Island   23
  9   Flagstaff Hill, Russell   23
10   Ruapekapeka Pa   24
11   Whale Bay, Tutukaka Coast   24
12   A. H. Reed Memorial Park, Whangarei   25
13   Bream Head/Te Whara   25
14   Smugglers Bay   25
15   Mt Manaia   26
16   Te Ara Manawa Walkway   26
17   North Head Sand Hill Formations   26
18   Arai te Uru Heritage Walkway   27
19   Waipoua Forest: Tane Mahuta   27
20   Waipoua Forest Kauri   28
21   Trounson Kauri Park   29
22   Kai Iwi Lakes Walkway   29
23   Tokatoka Peak   30
24   Waipu Caves   30
25   Tawharanui Regional Park   31

Auckland and Hauraki Gulf   32

1 Wenderholm Regional Park   33
2 Shakespear Regional Park   33
3 Okura Bush Walkway   34
4 North Head Historic Reserve   35
5 Muriwai Gannet Colony   36
6 Lake Wainamu   36
7 Cascade Kauri Park – City of Auckland Walk   37
8 Waitakere Dam   37
9 Fairy Falls   38
10 Whites Beach, Piha   38
11 Kitekite Falls   38
12 Nikau Grove, Piha   39
13 Tasman Lookout   39
14 Te Ahua Point   40
15 Whatipu Caves   41
16 Ninepin Rock and Paratutae   41
17 Historic Parnell   42
18 Mt Eden/Maungawhau   43
19 Cornwall Park and One Tree Hill Domain/Maungakiekie   44
20 Musick Point   45
21 Duder Regional Park   45
22 Tawhitokino Bay   46
23 Mangere Mountain   46
24 Auckland Botanic Gardens   47
25 Awhitu Regional Park   47
26 Hunua Falls   48
27 Waiheke: Stony Batter   48
28 Waiheke: School Loop Track, Whakanewha Regional Park   49
29 Waiheke: Matietie Historic Reserve   49
30 Kawau Island   50
31 Great Barrier Island: Kaitoke Hot Springs   51
32 Great Barrier Island: Windy Canyon   51

33 Rangitoto Island: McKenzie Bay and Lighthouse   51
34 Rangitoto Summit   52
35 Tiritiri Matangi   53

Coromandel   54

 1 Tokatea/Lucas Lookout   55
 2 Waiau Kauri Grove and Waterfall   55
 3 Square Kauri   56
 4 Kauaeranga Valley: Model Dam/Kahikatea Walk   56
 5 Kauaeranga Valley: Hoffman's Pool and Nature Walk   57
 6 Kauaeranga Valley: Edward's Lookout   57
 7 Opera Point   58
 8 Otama Beach   58
 9 Shakespeare Cliff and Lonely Bay   59
10 Hahei: Cathedral Cove   59
11 Hahei: Te Pare Historic Reserve   60
12 Tairua: Paku Peak   60
13 Mt Pauanui   61
14 Broken Hills: Gem of the Boom Creek   61
15 Broken Hills: Golden Hills Battery   61
16 Broken Hills: Collins Drive   62
17 Opoutere Beach   62
18 Wentworth Falls   63

Waikato and King Country   64

 1 Hamilton Gardens   65
 2 Jubilee Park   65
 3 Waikato River   66
 4 Miranda Shorebird Centre   66
 5 Karangahake Gorge: Historic Walkway Loop   67
 6 Karangahake Gorge: Windows   68

7 Mt Te Aroha: Whakapipi or Bald Spur   68

8 Howarth Memorial Wetland   69

9 Wairere Falls   69

10 Te Waihou Walkway   70

11 Te Koutu Lake   70

12 Hakarimata Scenic Reserve   71

13 Taupiri Mountain Summit   71

14 Bryant Memorial Scenic Reserve   72

15 Te Toto Gorge Scenic Reserve   72

16 Bridal Veil Falls   73

17 Mt Pirongia   73

18 Yarndley's Bush   74

19 Te Puia Hot Springs   74

20 Ruakuri Walkway   75

21 Mangapohue Natural Bridge   75

22 Marokopa Falls   76

23 Mangaokewa Gorge Scenic Reserve   76

24 Pureora Forest: Totara Walk   77

25 Pureora Forest: Buried Forest   77

26 Pureora Forest: Forest Tower Track   78

27 Poukani – the world's largest totara   78

28 Mapara Scenic Reserve   79

29 Omaru Falls   79

Bay of Plenty, Rotorua, Taupo and central North Island   80

1 Orokawa Bay   81

2 Bowentown Heads   81

3 Haiku Walk   82

4 Te Puna Quarry Park   82

5 Mt Maunganui/Mauao   83

6 Omanawa Falls   84

7 Papamoa Hills Regional Park Summit   85
8 Nga Tapuwae O Toi: Ohope to Otarawairere Beach   86
9 Nga Tapuwae O Toi: Kapu Te Rangi/Toi's Pa   86
10 Nga Tapuwae O Toi: Fairbrother Loop Walk   87
11 Historic Whakatane River   87
12 White Pine Bush   88
13 Ohiwa Harbour: Sandspit Wildlife Refuge   88
14 Tuwhare Pa   89
15 Hukutaia Domain/Burial Tree   89
16 Marawaiwai   90
17 Tauturangi Walkway   90
18 Rotorua City   91
19 Mokoia Island   92
20 The Redwoods/Whakarewarewa Forest   93
21 Okareka Walkway   93
22 Lake Tarawera   94
23 Blue and Green Lakes   94
24 Hinehopu's Track   95
25 Te Koutu Pa   95
26 Twin Craters/Ngahopua Track   96
27 Kerosene Creek   96
28 Rainbow Mountain/Maungakakaramea   97
29 Craters of the Moon   97
30 Huka Falls Walkway   97
31 Motuoapa Lookout   98
32 Thermal Tokaanu   99
33 Tongariro National Trout Centre   99
34 Lake Rotopounamu   100
35 Tongariro National Park: Taranaki Falls   100
36 Tongariro National Park: The Mounds   101
37 Tongariro National Park: Tawhai Falls   101

Hawke's Bay, Gisborne and East Cape 102

1 East Cape Lighthouse   103
2 Anaura Bay   103
3 Tolaga Bay Wharf   104
4 Cooks Cove Walkway   104
5 Makorori Point, Wainui Beach   105
6 Kaiti Hill, Gisborne   105
7 Gray's Bush   106
8 Waihirere Domain   106
9 Eastwoodhill Arboretum   107
10 Waikaremoana: Papakorito Falls   107
11 Waikaremoana: Whatapo Bay   107
12 Waikaremoana: Lou's Lookout   108
13 Waikaremoana: Lake Kiriopukae   108
14 Waikaremoana: Panekiri Bluff, First Trig   109
15 Morere Springs Scenic Reserve   109
16 Waiatai Reserve   110
17 Napier Botanical Gardens and Historic Cemetery   110
18 Whakamaharatanga Walkway   111
19 Maraetotara Falls Heritage Walk   111
20 Otatara Pa Historic Reserve   112
21 Te Mata Peak   112
22 Art Deco Napier   113
23 Napier: Marine Parade   114
24 Waikare Beach   115
25 Lake Tutira Wildlife Refuge and Country Park   116
26 Shine Falls   116
27 Opouahi Lake   117
28 Te Ana and Tangoio Falls   118
29 Waipatiki Reserve   118
30 Monckton Scenic Reserve   119
31 Lindsay Scenic Reserve   119
32 Mangatoro Scenic Reserve   120
33 Waihi Falls   120

Taranaki, Wanganui and Manawatu

Taranaki, Wanganui and Manawatu 121

1 Three Sisters and Elephant Rock 122
2 Mt Damper Falls 122
3 Te Henui Walkway 123
4 New Plymouth Coastal Walkway 123
5 Pukekura Park 124
6 Paritutu Rock 125
7 Koru Pa 125
8 North Egmont 126
9 Kapuni Loop Track to Dawson Falls 127
10 Lake Rotokare 128
11 Patea River 128
12 Bushy Park 129
13 Lake Virginia 129
14 Whanganui River 130
15 Historic Wanganui City 130
16 Mangaweka Scenic Reserve 131
17 Mangaweka Power Station 132
18 Pryce's Rahui Reserve 132
19 Sledge Track, Kahuterawa Valley 133
20 Victoria Esplanade 134
21 Savage Crescent 134
22 Wreck of the *Hyderabad* 135
23 Lake Papaitonga 135
24 Nikau Reserve 136
25 Waikanae River Estuary and Beach 136
26 Queen Elizabeth II Park 137

Wellington and Wairarapa

Wellington and Wairarapa 138

1 Castle Point 139
2 Lake Henley 139
3 Mt Holdsworth 140

4   Carter Scenic Reserve   141

5   Rapaki Hillside Walk   141

6   Ruakokopatuna Caves   142

7   Putangirua Pinnacles   142

8   Cape Palliser Lighthouse   143

9   Rimutaka Trig   141

10 Kaitoke Regional Park   143

11 Tunnel Gully, Tane's Track   144

12 Pauatahanui Wildlife Reserve   145

13 Belmont Trig   145

14 Korokoro Dam   146

15 Hutt River Trail   146

16 Butterfly Creek   147

17 Wellington Botanic Garden   147

18 Matiu/Somes Island   148

19 Mount Victoria   149

20 Wellington Waterfront   150

21 Wellington by Night   151

22 Zealandia: The Karori Sanctuary Experience   152

23 Otari–Wilton's Bush Native Botanic Garden and Forest Reserve 153

24 Makara Walkway   154

25 Café To Café   154

26 Red Rocks   155

Glossary of Maori terms   156

Introduction

For many years I've been a keen walker throughout New Zealand, but I often find that the longer trips, while enjoyable, are *too* much to tackle; for example, when I'm travelling or when I don't have the necessary gear to hand. And on many occasions I have visitors who are keen to 'get out and about' but do not have the time, experience or equipment for the longer trips.

I have discovered, however, that there are many excellent short walks to be found throughout the country, and that you don't have to tramp for hours to experience some of the best scenery or experiences New Zealand has to offer. This book is a collection of what I think are excellent short walks and encompass bush, coastal, urban and mountain country. Each walk has a highlight (or several highlights) so you can pick and choose to suit your tastes and time. No special gear is necessary, the walks are not hard to find, and you won't get lost. You will not need to take food or water, though in summer on some of the longer walks water will be appreciated, and an energy bar or two never goes amiss.

So whether you are eight years old or eighty, these walks should suit almost everyone. Now all you have to do is to stop the car, get out and get walking!

How to use this book

It's worth pointing out that *Excellent Short Walks in the North Island* is intended to be a fund of ideas rather than a blow-by-blow track guide. The brevity of the walks removes the need for detailed track notes, and any walks that were hard to follow have not been included. Some authorities are great with signage, others are hopeless, while some don't take visitors into account and just assume that walkers are local and know where to go. However, I have been reluctant to be too critical regarding poor signage as signs have often been destroyed or vandalised, rather than not existing in the first place. Authorities must be constantly disheartened by defaced information boards, smashed signs and wrecked direction boards.

Point of interest ✳

Each walk has as its destination a point of interest. In some cases this will be a true ruby in the dust – a hidden gem among otherwise unremarkable surroundings – while in others, particularly the more remote and scenic spots, you may be spoilt for choice.

How to get there ➤

These descriptions assume that the traveller has a reasonable road atlas and, in urban areas, a street map. The excellent network of Information Centres and Department of Conservation offices will be able to help out if you don't have a local map or are really unsure of directions.

Grade 𝝆

Easy   Can be managed by almost everyone; mainly flat to rolling, and generally in good condition. However, these walks can include steps, short steep sections, a bit of mud and the occasional rough patch.

Medium   Will include rough stretches, muddy patches and steps or steep sections.

Hard   In short this really means steep. These walks will require a bit of fitness and a bit of uphill sweat.

Time

The times given are conservative and assume a very leisurely pace. A fit person can expect to take 25 to 30 per cent less time than stated.

The times given on information boards also tend to be very conservative. Don't be put off by what seems a long walk – they are usually much shorter.

Gear

No special gear is required for these walks, but New Zealand weather is notoriously fickle and unpredictable, and the conditions of the tracks vary considerably, so be prepared.

Shoes: Tramping boots are not necessary, but you will be much more comfortable with a good pair of trainers that you don't mind getting dirty and that have good tread. Tracks are often muddy or have slippery sections over rocks and wooden steps.

Jacket: Invest in a rain-proof jacket. Many jackets are only shower- or wind-proof, and it rains a lot in New Zealand. If you don't want to go to the expense, then those heavy yellow plastic coats may not be elegant bushwear, but they are cheap and certainly keep the rain out. In wetter seasons having a few dry clothes in the car is a good idea so if you do get wet you have something warm to change into.

A word about jandals

Jandals are as Kiwi as it gets, but they are absolutely hopeless on walking tracks. Once your feet are wet you will slip out of them easily, and in the wet they flick mud up the back of your legs. Even worse, you are likely to snap the thong and break your very best jandals, which is very distressing. If you don't like shoes, there are now plenty of strong sandals that have good tread and offer good support.

Security

An unfortunate fact of life in modern New Zealand is that car burglary is now common in walk car parks. Some very popular attractions now even have security guards. Short of leaving someone with the car at all times, there are a few things you can do to lessen the chances of having your car broken into. Lock your car even on the short walks, and double-check that your windows are closed (it is easy to forget your back windows). Make sure that all valuables are out of sight, and if possible carry your most valuable items with you (wallet, camera, phone, video). Invest in an inexpensive steering lock: this won't stop your car being broken into, but it will indicate to thieves that you are security-conscious and it will almost certainly stop them actually stealing the car.

Mobile phones

Mobile phones can be very useful if you are lost, but be aware they do not always have coverage in some of the more remote places.

Acknowledgements

Many thanks to all the folks at Information Centres and DoC offices who have not only been very helpful but also very enthusiastic and supportive. Also thanks to those people who have helped in many ways including Alexei Kondaurov for his information on godwits.

Finally a thanks to patient editors and the staff at New Holland, who have backed this project from the beginning.

Northland

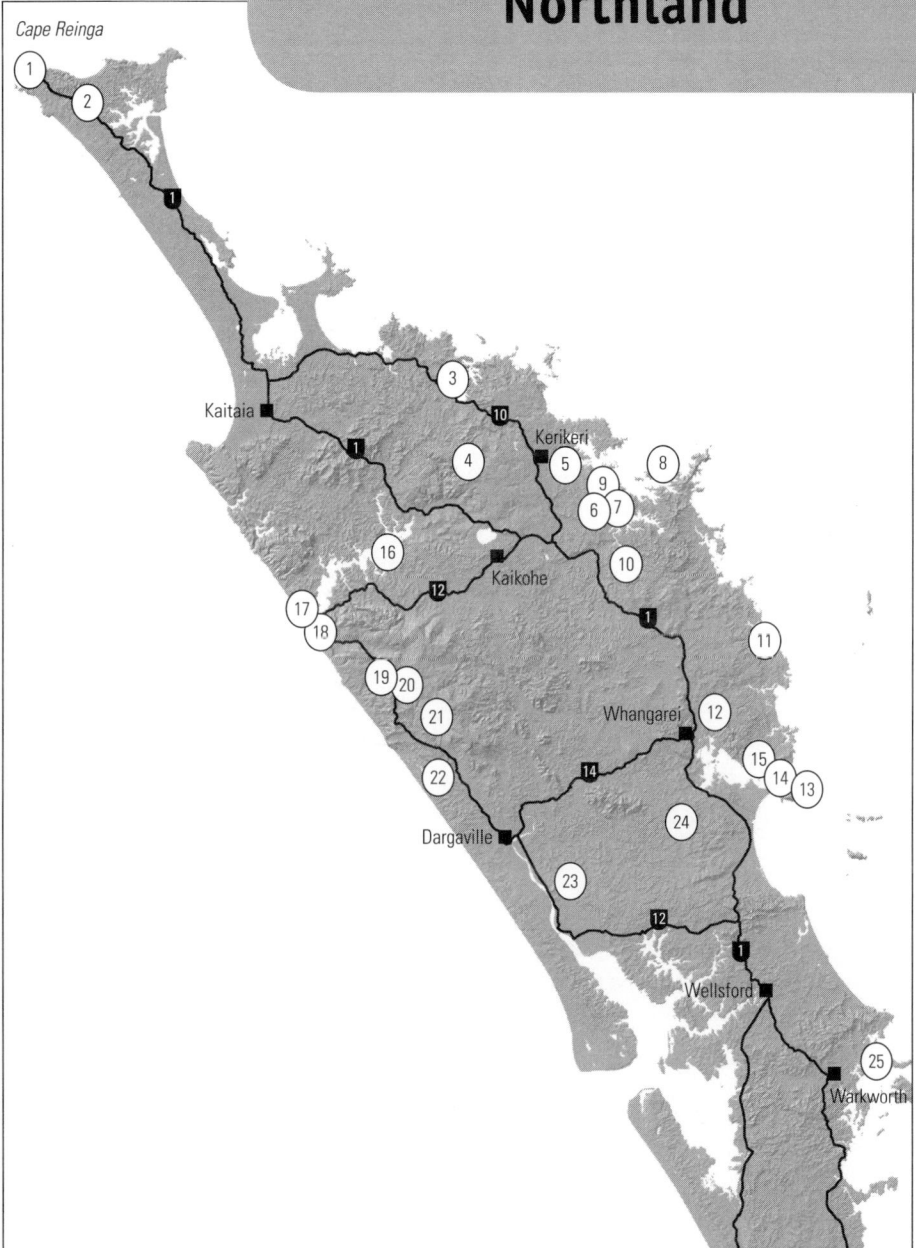

Cape Reinga

Kaitaia

Kerikeri

Kaikohe

Whangarei

Dargaville

Wellsford

Warkworth

1 Cape Reinga

✳ Spectacular cape with deep spiritual importance to Maori.

➤ This is the very end of SH1: you can't go any further.

The following three walks all leave from the car park at the cape.

Cape Reinga Lighthouse   Easy   🚶 20 minutes return

Often described, mistakenly, as the most northerly point of the New Zealand mainland (that honour belongs to Surville Cliffs at North Cape), Cape Reinga is renowned for the spectacular and wild seascapes of the Columbia Bank where the Tasman Sea and the Pacific Ocean meet. In Maori tradition the cape is the final departing point for the spirits of the dead on their journey to the underworld domain of Hine-nui-te-Po, the goddess of death. The twisted and gnarled vegetation along the coast is where the spirits have desperately attempted to cling to this world. The importance of this site to Maori has kept the area free from commercialisation, though it does get very crowded in the middle of the day with bus tours.

The lighthouse, constructed in 1941, was the last staffed lighthouse to be built in the country. An easy walk on a sealed path leads down to it.

Te Werahi Beach   Medium   🚶 1½ hours return

While people flock to the cape, most visitors rarely venture further afield than the lighthouse. The magnificent Te Werahi Beach on the western side of the cape is not too far away, and yet there is a good chance you will have the beach to yourself. The walk begins along spectacular coastal cliffs that drop hundreds of metres to the rocks below. The salt-laden spray from the wild waves produces bonsai-like manuka, and diminutive pohutukawa and flax cling to the cliffs. From the cliff-top the track winds down through a sheltered valley to broad sandy Te Werahi Beach.

Sandfly Bay   Hard   🚶 1½ hours return

On the northern side of the cape, a steep track descends from the car park through wind-ravaged flora to a small sandy cove that is only reached by foot. The track continues on to Tapotupotu where there is an excellent beach and camping ground.

2 Te Paki Sand Hills Medium 🚶 1 hour

* Huge golden sand hills over 150 metres high rise above Te Paki Stream.

➤ Te Paki Stream Road, off the Cape Reinga road.

These massive sand dunes stretch from Te Paki Stream to Te Werahi Beach, in places reaching as high as 150 metres. The light gold sand blends with the yellowy-green dune-creeper pingao, which manages to take hold in the shifting sands. Sand-surfing on boogie boards is a popular activity here, and there are a number of places hiring out boards, including one right at the car park during the summer.

The best way to walk the sand hills is to start walking from the car park up the loose sand of the dunes. This is hard work; when you have had enough drop down to Te Paki Stream, which is both flat and shallow, and an easy walk back to the car park. Te Paki Stream serves as a major access route to Ninety Mile Beach, so keep an eye out for speeding vehicles.

3 St Paul's Rock, Whangaroa Harbour Hard 🚶 45 minutes

* Magnificent views of the Whangaroa Harbour from high up on this old volcanic cone.

➤ Take the turn-off to Whangaroa on SH10 north of Kaeo. Turn right onto Old Hospital Road 500 metres past the Marlin Hotel and before the main wharf. The track begins at the road end. Despite the signs warning of limited parking and turnaround space, there is in fact good parking and an easy turnaround just 50 metres beyond the beginning of the track.

For those familiar with the tidal upper Whangaroa Harbour, the beauty of this bush-clad and almost enclosed bay will be a pleasant surprise. The views are spectacular of the fiord-like harbour far below, stretching out to the narrow entrance and beyond where Stephenson Island is clearly visible. The barren rock is an old pa site and the evidence of middens is everywhere, though why early Maori wanted to lug shellfish all the way up here for their tea when they could have eaten them down by the sea is anyone's guess.

The track is a rough uphill climb, and the last section is a rocky scramble to the top, though chain handrails assist in the steepest places.

4 Puketi Kauri Forest   Easy   🚶 20 minutes

* A short circular walk through magnificent mature kauri.

➤ The forest entrance is 13 km along the Puketi Road (unsealed) between Okaihau and Kerikeri.

While other forests contain larger trees, this 20,000-hectare reserve gives the visitor a feel of the great kauri forests of the past. The Manginangina kauri walk is a short boardwalk that loops through huge mature trees which offer visitors a true appreciation of this iconic New Zealand tree. Nearby longer tracks lead much deeper into the forest.

5 Kerikeri Basin   Easy

* Two of New Zealand's oldest buildings and an historic pa site combine with a delightful river walk.

➤ At the end of Kerikeri Road, Kerikeri; well signposted from SH10.

🚶 Historic Power Station: 30 minutes return
Wharepuke Falls: 40 minutes return
Fairy Pools: 1 hour 10 minutes return
Rainbow Falls: 2 hours return
Rainbow Falls from Rainbow Falls Road off Waipapa Road: 15 minutes return
Kororipo Pa: 20 minutes return

The Kemp House (built 1821) and the Stone Store (built 1835) in the historic Kerikeri Mission Station are New Zealand's oldest buildings. They sit side by side in the Kerikeri Basin, which was as far upriver as boats could go before striking rapids. More importantly, they were built near Kororipo pa, the home of one of the most powerful chiefs in the north, Hongi Hika. Without Hongi Hika's patronage and protection, the mission had little chance of survival.

From the car park over the river from the historic buildings, a walk wends its way up the Kerikeri River as far as Rainbow Falls. If you don't have someone to pick you up at the falls you will need to return the same way. The walk follows the pretty river through attractive bush and rocky bluffs, and the track is in excellent condition. The Power Station began operation in 1930 supplying just 17 households. The simple machinery is now protected by a modern shed that also houses information and historic photos. A large intake pipe, partly buried in the ground, disappears up the hill towards where the water was originally supplied from a weir above the falls.

Wharepuke Falls is a picturesque waterfall that drops into a popular swimming hole, while further upstream the Fairy Pools are two large swimming holes. The Fairy Pools have a large picnic area that is also accessed off Kerikeri Road. Access from this side is down a short but rough lane followed by a walk through mature eucalyptus. At the time of writing, this very pretty area was unfortunately a bit scruffy and rubbish-strewn.

At Rainbow Falls the Kerikeri River drops an impressive 27 metres into a large deep pool. Behind the falls is a large cave where the action of water has worn away the rock behind the falling water. Rainbow Falls is also accessible from Rainbow Falls Road. Here a short track leads to the right from the car park to three lookout points high above the falls; a track to the left of the car park leads down to the pool at the bottom of the falls.

Kororipo pa is on the other side of the river from the car park, and the walk begins alongside the Basin. This pa was Hongi Hika's main stronghold, superbly positioned on a bend in the river. The fortifications are clearly visible and, with an uninterrupted view back to the Kemp House and the Stone Store, it is clear that the Nga Puhi chief would have been able to keep a good eye on the comings and goings of the Pakeha living there. The excellent interpretive panels give the visitor a good idea of life in this pa two centuries ago.

With no handy beach nearby, the river is a popular place to go swimming and along its length has numerous swimming holes. Just 5 minutes from the car park is a spot in the river right behind the sign 'Warning/Hazard. Don't swim if the river is in flood'.

The middle section of the walk from Wharepuke Falls to just below the Rainbow Falls is closed until May 2008 while a bypass is under construction.

6 Mangroves, Waitangi   Easy   🚶 1½ hours one way

* A boardwalk wends its way through an old mangrove forest.

➤ The Waitangi end begins on the left by the golf course just past the Treaty House; the Haruru Falls end is off Puketona Road.

This popular walk links regenerating bush alongside the mangrove estuary with the Haruru Falls, where the Waitangi River drops into a wide pool. The highlight of the walk is the long boardwalk that snakes through an old mangrove forest. Although mangroves grow as far south as Opotiki, it is here in the warm northern waters that they attain their maximum height. The estuary mud is thick with the aerial roots of these old trees, with their white and grey bark and tough small leaves. Mangrove swamps are now recognised as vital environments in maintaining water quality and provide a perfect hideaway nursery for young fish.

Unfortunately it is not easy to shorten this walk as the boardwalk through the mangroves is equidistant from both ends of the walk. It is worth the effort to organise a pick-up at the other end if you are not keen on walking there and back.

7 Paihia Lookout   Easy   🚶 1 hour return

* Pleasant views over Paihia, Russell and the Bay of Islands.

➤ 750 metres along School Road, Paihia.

The track begins along a picturesque stream overhung with a tangle of nikau palms, ferns and ropey supplejack with some good-sized totara and puriri. As the track climbs, the dense bush gives way to drier soils with manuka and kanuka bushes and, near the lookout, young kauri (or rickers). The lookout has views through a broad arc taking in Waitangi, Paihia, Russell and Opua as well as out over the bay. This is a lovely quiet place and ideal to tackle in the cool of the morning or the early evening to get away from the bustle of the Paihia waterfront. Keep an eye out for fantails, tits and robins flitting in the trees alongside the track.

Although uphill the grade is very even and the track is well formed. About 20 minutes into the walk, the track reaches an unmarked junction: the track to the lookout continues to the right.

8 Urupukapuka Island   Easy   🚶   2 hours

* A small island in the heart of the bay, with sheltered beaches and old pa sites.

➤ How to get there: Several operators run trips out to the island in the summer months. The i-Site on the Paihia Wharf will have up-to-date information.

A series of easy walking tracks links a number of small sandy beaches on this island on the outer reaches of the bay. It was at Otehei Bay (where the ferry lands) that the legendary American fisherman Zane Grey had his base. Famous as a writer of pulp westerns and the creator of the Lone Ranger, Grey lived here in 1926, fishing for marlin, broadbill and shark. His book *Tales of an Angler's Eldorado* put the Bay of Islands on the map as a fishing destination for the rich and famous.

There is also a café and overnight accommodation on the island. Since the ferry's maximum capacity is 30, the number of people on the island is always limited.

9 Flagstaff Hill, Russell   Medium   🚶   45 minutes return

* An historic site with good views over the Bay of Islands.

➤ From the north end of the beach at Russell continue past the boat ramp and along the rocky shore to the beginning of the track.

As tensions grew between the Maori and British during the 1840s, Nga Puhi chief Hone Heke was well aware of the symbolic nature of the British flag flying over Russell. Four times he cut down the flagpole above the town, despite extensive British attempts to protect it. After the fourth time, the town itself was attacked and captured by Hone Heke. Today a modern flagpole still stands here, and the view over the Bay of Islands and Russell is impressive.

The coastal part of the walk is tide-dependent, so it is best to start with this part and avoid having to return uphill if you find yourself cut off by the tide. The track winds up through regenerating bush; at Titore Way turn right and then take the track uphill to the flagstaff. On the return trip, walk down to the car park and then take the steps down to Wellington Street, which leads back to town.

10 Ruapekapeka Pa   Easy   𝕏   45 minutes return

* A well-preserved pa site that was both innovative and effective in Maori resistance to British military might.

➤ 35 km north of Whangarei on SH1, turn right at Towai into Ruapekapeka Road. The pa site is 4 km down this road, which is unsealed and narrow in places.

This pa was the site of the final battle in the war of the north in 1845. The British, outnumbering the Maori three to one, were confounded by Kawiti's innovative defences which, unlike traditional pa fortifications, featured underground bunkers and foxholes to protect the defenders from cannon and musket fire. The pa fell only when the Maori, believing the British would not attack on a Sunday, were caught off guard and were forced to abandon it.

The pa site has great views over the surrounding countryside. Note that the car park is a little way from the site, and the British position is not be confused with the actual pa, the entrance of which is marked by a fine carved gateway. The outline of the pa is very clear and complemented by good information boards.

11 Whale Bay, Tutukaka Coast   Easy   𝕏   30 minutes return

* Views looking out over Woolleys Bay from a small sandy bay overhung with pohutukawa.

➤ Well signposted to the right at the top of the hill just north of Matapouri.

A short walk leads down through puriri, pohutukawa and a fine grove of nikau to a small cove that is everything you could wish a beach to be. Overhung with old trees, ideal for a shady picnic on a hot summer's day, the beach of fine white sandy is ideal for swimming, and both the track and beach have excellent views along the wide sweep of Woolleys Bay to the north.

There is a track out to the headland, and Whale Bay can be accessed by foot from the northern end of Matapouri Bay.

12 A. H. Reed Memorial Park   Easy   ﹅   40 minutes return

✸ A well-preserved reserve of mature bush including kauri.

➤ Whareroa Road, which is off the end of Mill Road, Whangarei.

Bordered by the Hatea River, this park contains several large kauri, some up to 500 years old. Named after pioneer publisher Alfred Reed, the park also contains fine stands of totara and a waterfall.

13 Bream Head/Te Whara   Medium   ﹅   1¾ hours return

✸ A secret radar station with magnificent coastal views.

➤ The track begins at the beach access car park at Ocean Beach, 40 km from Whangarei and 3 km from Urquharts Bay.

Named Te Whara by Maori after Manaia's principal wife, and Bream Head by Captain Cook when he mistook tarakihi for bream, this coastal reserve contains rare flora and fauna including such birds as kiwi, kaka, and red-crowned kakariki (New Zealand parakeets). During the Second World War a top-secret surveillance station was established on Bream Head with radar to scan the waters to the north and warn of any possible attack. This was after the RMS *Niagara* struck a German mine off Bream Head in June 1940; although no lives were lost, a large amount of gold sank with the ship.

Ocean Beach below the head is a magnificent sweep of sandy beach renowned for its surf. It's just the place for a swim after a hot uphill walk.

14 Smugglers Bay   Easy   ﹅   40 minutes return

✸ A stunning sandy beach with views out to the outer islands of the Hauraki Gulf.

➤ The track begins at the car park at the very end of Urquharts Bay Road.

This beautiful white-sand beach, overhung with pohutukawa, is not just a colourful name but an actual smugglers' hideout where early Scots settlers smuggled crates of whisky ashore to avoid customs. On Busby Head overlooking the bay is an ancient pa site, and on the headland on the harbour side are the remains of a Second World War gun emplacement.

15 Mt Manaia   Hard   🚶 2 hours return

✳ The rocky outcrops of Mt Manaia offer great views of the Whangarei area.

➤ From the city take Riverside Drive out towards Whangarei Heads. The track starts from the car park of the Mt Manaia Club, 30 km from the city.

This distinctive mountain (460 metres) is easily recognised by the numerous volcanic outcrops that define the peak. In Maori legend the rocky peaks are the figures of the rangatira Manaia, his two daughters and his wife, pursued by the chief from whom Manaia stole his wife; all were turned to stone by the god of thunder. From the top the views are spectacular in all directions. Keep an eye out for kaka parrots in the bush leading up to the peak.

16 Te Ara Manawa Walkway   Easy   🚶 20 minutes return

✳ A boardwalk through huge mangroves and the site of an old sawmill.

➤ Clendon Esplanade on the eastern side of Rawene township.

Mangroves are a common feature of shallow northern harbours, but only in the Far North do they grow to the size of small trees. Usually associated with the tropics, the single New Zealand species *Avicennia marina* subspecies *australiasica* is the southernmost in the world; in recent years, with the warmer weather, this species has been rapidly expanding its range. Excellent information boards make this a fascinating walk at any tide.

17 North Head Sand Hill Formations
Medium   🚶 1½ hours return to the formations

✳ Massive sand hills, shaped into deep gullies and cliffs by wind and rain.

➤ Hokianga Express Charters (phone 09 405 8872) runs a water taxi from Opononi wharf on the hour, depending on demand.

On the seaward side of these golden sand hills a combination of wind and rain have shaped the hard sand into deep gullies and wind-blasted cliffs and formations. These sand hills are much larger close up than they appear from a distance, and walking on the sand can be a strain – don't be too ambitious. The hills are also exposed to harsh winds, so make sure you take plenty of water in hot weather and thick clothing in cooler weather.

18 Arai te Uru Heritage Walkway Easy 人 20 minutes return

* ✸ Spectacular coastal scenery both to the north and inland along the Hokianga Harbour.

* ➤ Signal Station Road off SH12, 4 km west of Omapere.

This short walk on the South Head of the Hokianga Harbour winds through wind-stunted manuka, flax and toetoe. It has incredible views north over the giant golden sand hills on the northern shore, and east along the inland waterway that is Hokianga Harbour. Discovered by Kupe, the Hokianga winds a surprisingly long way inland: SH1 crosses the Hokianga at Mangamuka Bridge. The hard sandy soil has been shaped by persistent wind, and below the lookout is a lovely sandy cove that can be accessed by a well-defined but unmarked track that starts at the car park.

19 Waipoua Forest: Tane Mahuta Easy 人 5 minutes return

* ✸ Tane Mahuta is New Zealand's tallest kauri tree.

* ➤ SH12, 53 km north of Dargaville.

Rising to a height of 51.5 metres, Tane Mahuta or Lord of the Forest is the country's tallest kauri. It is very easy to access via a short loop track through native bush that starts by a bridge over a picturesque stream. Impressive trees were recorded in historic time measuring twice this size; and a visit to the Matakohe Kauri Museum will give the visitor a new appreciation of these giants of the forest.

20 Waipoua Forest Kauri Easy

✳ A real appreciation of the magnificent presence of kauri forest rather than an isolated tree or two.

➤ The car park is 1 km south of Tane Mahuta, on SH12.

🚶 Four Sisters: 15 minutes return

Te Matua Ngahere: 45 minutes return

Yakas Kauri: 1 hour 10 minutes return

These three walks all start from the same track from the car park. A small fee is charged for parking security.

Four Sisters. A rare example of a four-headed kauri sprouting from a single base. Although not all the trunks are the same size, they are all impressive trees in their own right.

Te Matua Ngahere. The second-largest kauri tree. This tree has a much greater girth than Tane Mahuta – 16.4 metres compared with Tane's 13 metres. Although not as tall, and with branches starting much lower down than Tane Mahuta, Te Matua Ngahere or Father of the Forest sits deeper within the forest and appears much larger.

Yakas Kauri. At first glance it seems mean-spirited to refer to this tree as 'the seventh-largest kauri' and might seem easy to give this walk a miss. However, what makes this particular walk appealing is that it passes through some magnificent groves of huge kauri trees that give a much greater appreciation of the beauty of this forest, most of which has long disappeared.

Night Walks. An Opononi company offers a night tour that is a unique combination of Maori culture and natural history. The walking is easy and the walking part of the tour is about 2 hours. For information see www.footprintswaipoua.com.

21 Trounson Kauri Park   Easy   🏃   45 minutes (loop)

✴ A mature kauri forest that is also a 'mainland island', an area with special environmental protection.

➤ Trounson can be accessed by a 15 km loop road clearly marked from SH12 south of Waipoua.

This forest remnant was set aside as reserve by local landowner James Trounson. It was officially opened as Trounson Kauri Park in 1921 and now covers over 450 hectares of virgin kauri forest. The loop walk is through impressive groves of mature kauri with an understorey of nikau, fern and kiekie; with fewer visitors than nearby Waipoua, the forest retains a quiet and primeval feel. The forest is also a 'mainland island' reserve where intense control of predators has seen a recovery of many species including kiwi and kereru (New Zealand pigeon).

22 Kai Iwi Lakes Walkway
Easy   🏃   2 hours return (1 hour if you have someone to pick you up at the other end)

✴ These dune lakes have beautiful azure water lapping fine white sandy beaches.

➤ The road to Kai Iwi Lakes is clearly marked from SH12, 20 km north of Dargaville. The walk begins at the northern end of the camp ground.

The Kai Iwi lakes are a series of deep lakes, the deepest and largest of which, Taharoa, drops to a depth of 37 metres. What makes these lakes so appealing is that the water is of a deepest blue in the middle shading through to azure, tropical-hued shallows, which lap beaches of fine white sand.

The walk follows the northern shore of Taharoa; if you don't have a ride organised you can return the same way or via the road. The kindest comment to make about the vegetation around the lake is that it has been 'severely compromised'. The lakes are also popular with boaties and water skiers, so at times the noise level can be rather high. There is a large camping area here, but this is a popular place to pitch a tent so if you plan to stay, book ahead.

23 Tokatoka Peak Medium ☂ 40 minutes return

✳ Fantastic views over the Wairoa River from this old volcanic core.

➤ At Tokatoka Tavern, on SH12 north of Ruawai, turn right into Tokatoka Road.
The track begins about 1.5 km on the left by the 'Scenic Reserve' sign.

Tokatoka Peak is the hardened lava core of an old volcano, from which the outer volcanic material has eroded away. Its distinctive shape is impossible to miss on the road from Ruawai to Dargaville. From a distance the peak looks quite difficult to climb; in fact the ascent from the eastern side is not that hard, though the track, through regenerating bush, is not well formed and it is a bit of a scramble near the top. The scramble is well worth the effort, as the views from the summit are superb. Below, the languid Wairoa River snakes through the flat landscape as it wends its way south to Kaipara Harbour. To the east the views are inland to rugged bush-clad ranges, while right below the peak, sitting on a bluff alongside the river, is the distinct shape of an old pa site, ideally situated both for protection and to keep an eye on the comings and goings on the river.

24 Waipu Caves Easy ☂ 20 minutes return

✳ A limestone cave with glow-worms.

➤ About 13 km off SH1. Turn-offs are clearly signposted at several points between Waipu and Whangarei. The last 5 km of the road is unsealed and narrow.

This cave system, just a short walk from the road, features limestone formations, stalactites and stalagmites, and is one of the best glow-worm caves in the country. A torch is essential as the caves are quite deep. It is necessary to wade through shallow water to see the glow-worms, which are about 100 metres to the left from the cave entrance.

25 Tawharanui Regional Park   Medium

✴ Magnificent vistas of the Hauraki Gulf and especially Little Barrier Island are combined with beautiful sandy beaches.

➤ The park is clearly signposted from 26 km out of Warkworth on SH1. The last 5 km of road just before the park is unsealed, narrow and winding.

🚶 Tokatu Point: 2 hours return

Ecology Trail: 1½ hours return

Comprising almost 600 hectares of rolling farmland and bushy gullies, the Tawharanui Peninsula juts out into the Hauraki Gulf, with Little Barrier Island looming to the north and wooded Kawau Island just to the south. Almost the entire northern shore is protected as the Tawharanui Marine Park.

The rolling hills make for easy walking, and the open nature of the park affords constant views from almost every point. A predator-proof fence makes this park a haven for native birds.

The magnificent sweep of Anchor Bay, north-facing and sheltered from the south-westerly winds, is an ideal base for two short walks, though the park is a maze of tracks and there is plenty of scope for those wanting a longer walk. The dune area behind the bay is roped off in spring to protect the breeding ground of the rare New Zealand dotterel.

The Tokatu Point lookout walk starts from the eastern side of the car park at Anchor Bay. The views of the gulf along this walk are spectacular and it is worthwhile taking a short detour on the Tokatu Loop track to view rare prostrate manuka.

The Ecology Trail can be shortened by returning along the North Coast trail, making a loop trip of around 45 minutes. This walk follows both beach and rocky shore, and then heads inland to meander through a patch of mature bush before returning to the car park. Start this trip by walking onto the beach from the Anchor Bay car park, and then follow the markers along the coast.

Auckland and Hauraki Gulf

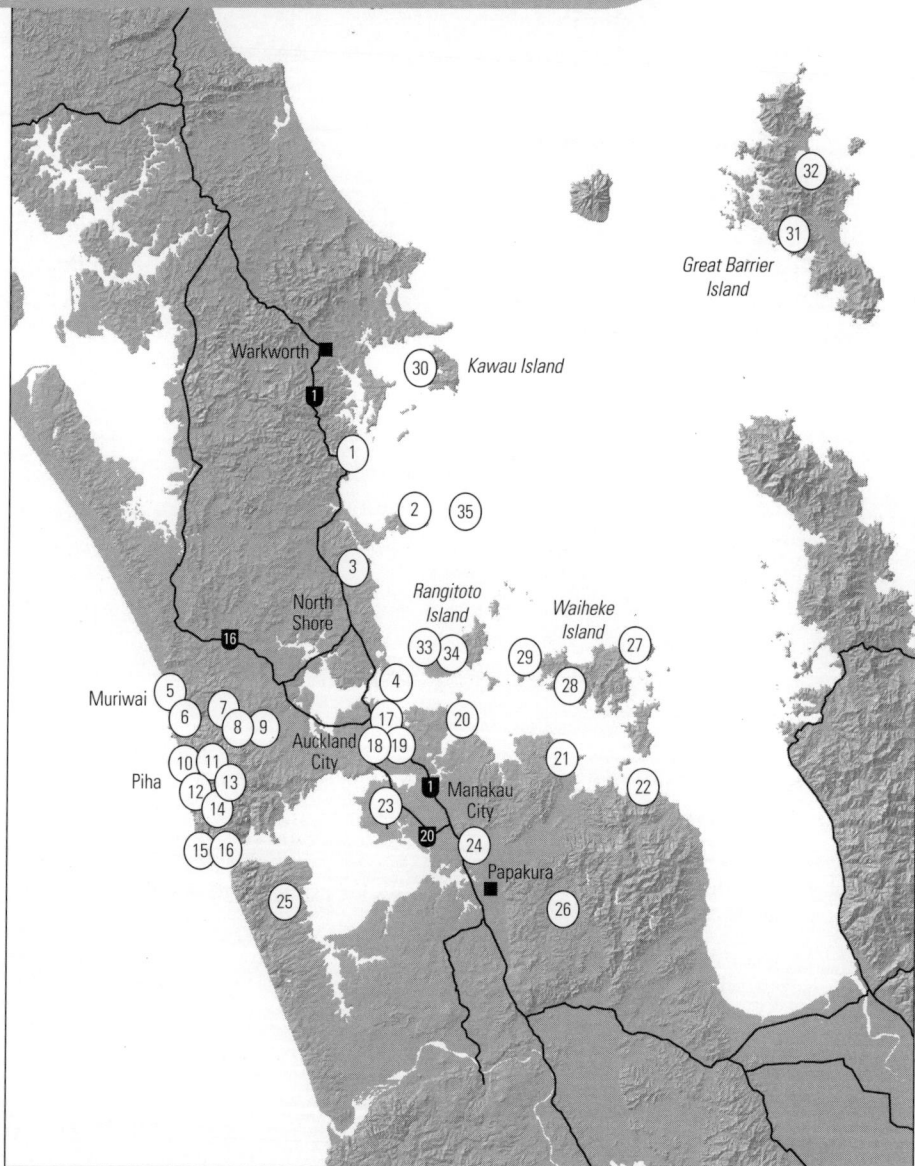

Warkworth

Kawau Island

Great Barrier Island

North Shore

Rangitoto Island

Waiheke Island

Muriwai

Auckland City

Piha

Manakau City

Papakura

1 Wenderholm Regional Park Medium

✳ A beautiful pohutakawa-lined beach and bush walk with great views of the Hauraki Gulf.

➤ On SH1, 1 km north of Waiwera.

⅄ Lookout: 45 minutes return

Perimeter walk: 2 hours

Combining a fine sandy beach, an historic homestead and a bush walk, Wenderholm Regional Park, between the Puhoi and Waiwera rivers, is an ideal family destination for a day out. Wenderholm, meaning 'winter home', was an earlier name of the historic house built around 1857 and now known as Couldrey House. The house is open from 1 pm to 4 pm on Saturday and Sunday all year round, and every afternoon between Boxing Day and Waitangi weekend (early February). Right behind the house a track leads up through a fine stand of native bush to a great viewpoint over the Hauraki Gulf.

The track to the lookout is well formed. It is a steady uphill climb through mature native bush containing, thanks to recent predator control, a surprising number of native birds including tui, kereru (New Zealand pigeon) and fantails. Beyond the lookout the track drops steeply (and is very rough and muddy even in summer) to the Waiwera River and then continues along the river to the road and then back to the beach. An alternative that avoids the noisy road section is to take the track through the middle of the park up to a fine lookout over Waiwera, and then back to the beach on a steep downhill.

2 Shakespear Regional Park Easy

✳ Views of the Hauraki Gulf, sandy beaches and old gun emplacements.

➤ From SH1 at Silverdale just south of Orewa turn into Whangaparaoa Road and follow the signs to the very end of the peninsula. Park at the car park by the small lake, a short distance south of Army Bay.

⅄ 45 minutes return to the Lookout, and 1 hour 15 minutes to Te Haruhi Bay via the Lookout.

Located at the tip of the Whangaparaoa Peninsula, this park is a very attractive combination of bush, beach, history and great views. The area just north of the park is still Ministry of Defence land, but within the park are a number of historic pillboxes constructed as part of an elaborate defence network north of Auckland. (Pillboxes were low concrete structures, often partially dug into the ground and designed to house machine guns or antitank guns.) Now protected by a predator-proof fence, bird life will only improve in the years to come, especially given the close proximity of Tiritiri Matangi Island.

Following the Heritage Trail the walk steadily climbs uphill through a deep bush valley, then open farmland, to the Lookout. The views are superb along the coast to the north, out to the islands of the Gulf and south to downtown Auckland. From here take the Lookout Track downhill to Te Haruhi Bay, a small sandy beach lined with pohutukawa. From the beach, the Lookout Track continues uphill, passing an old shearing shed built around 1900. The track rejoins the Heritage Trail, which then meets the fence, from where it leads back to the car park.

The park's name is not a spelling mistake, but recalls an early farming family with the surname Shakespear.

3 Okura Bush Walkway Easy

✸ A very fine grove of mature puriri.

➤ Drive north on East Coast Road from its intersection with Oteha Valley Road; after 4.5 km turn right into Haighs Access Road. The track begins at the end of the road.

Grove: 45 minutes return
Sandspit in the river: 1½ hours

While the walk to Dacre Cottage is 4 hours return, the puriri grove at the beginning of the track is worth a visit in its own right, and this initial section contains the best of the native bush on the walk. Puriri is a very handsome native tree, with glossy leaves, a broad spreading habit, and attractive small purple-red flowers that often carpet the forest floor beneath the tree. Puriri is unusual in that it flowers and fruits all year round. The trunk is short and is often full of hollows, and is home to the native puriri moth.

The track through the grove is well formed. When you reach the top of a ridge marked by an old fence post, return the way you came. Alternatively, continue on another 45 minutes return to a sandspit in the Okura River, which is home to shore and wading birds. From this point the bush is mainly regrowth with more mature trees in the gully and the occasional kauri.

4 North Head Historic Reserve

Easy 🚶 15 minutes return from the car park to the disappearing gun, but allow at least 1 hour to explore.

✳ Wide views over the Waitemata Harbour from this sea-fringed volcanic cone with fortifications including tunnels and gun emplacements.

➤ The main vehicle entrance is at the end of Takarunga Road, Cheltenham. North Head is about a 20-minute walk from Devonport Wharf.

The North Head reserve occupies the ancient and prominent cone of Maungauika, which stands sentinel over the inner Waitemata Harbour. Curiously, although there is evidence of occupation and cultivation of the rich volcanic soil, Maungauika was not fortified by Maori in pre-European times. Nearby Takarunga/Mt Victoria was the main pa for the area.

As early as 1836 a pilot station was established at the foot of North Head. In 1885, in response to the Russian expansion into the Pacific, the government set about building three batteries to protect the city from an imminent attack (the explosion of Mt Tarawera in 1886 was initially thought to be the beginning of a Russian bombardment). The underground tunnels and the oldest buildings on the summit, a cookhouse and barracks, still remain from this period. Further fortifications were added during both the First and Second World Wars and the reserve has excellent signage including original photographs of the defence positions.

The south battery is still intact. It features one of the few disappearing guns left in the world; although it is no longer working, it was designed to be loaded underground, raised and then fired, thereby protecting the men servicing the gun.

While most people visiting North Head walk from the car park to the disappearing gun, it is worth taking more time to explore the area. The cookhouse on the summit (open 8.30 am to 4 pm) has a collection of old photos and shows a short video, while there are extensive rooms and tunnels just below the summit on the eastern side.

A track around the base of the cone leads to small sea caves and a sheltered sandy cove suitable for swimming (also accessible from Cheltenham Beach over the rocks). North Head is also a popular spot for a bit of rock fishing, as the main channel runs close to the shore at this point.

5 Muriwai Gannet Colony Easy 𝕏 30 minutes return

✳ A rare close-up view of a gannet colony.

➤ End of Motutara Road, Muriwai.

Early in the 20th century Australasian gannets began establishing nesting sites on Oaia Island (which lies 1.5 km offshore), then on Motutara Island, and in 1979 they established themselves on Otakamiro Point, one of only two mainland nesting sites in New Zealand. Now each year, from August to April, over 1200 pairs nest here and the proximity of the nesting birds gives the public easy and close access. The best time to see the chicks is November and December.

Fur seals can also be seen on Oaia Island.

6 Lake Wainamu Easy 𝕏 1 hour return

✳ A massive sand dune blocks the Wainamu stream, creating a deep lake.

➤ The track begins on the left once you cross the bridge about 1 km before Bethells Beach/Te Henga.

The track follows the stream initially, and then climbs the huge sand dune to the lake. The dune is much bigger than it first appears and in a strong westerly wind the sand is whipped across the broad dune, like some desolate desert scene from a movie. The lake at the edge of the dune is particularly deep and is an ideal swimming spot. To return, follow the lake edge to the left and then stroll back to the car park via the shallow stream. Children and the young at heart will have great fun sliding down the steep dunes along the stream.

7 Cascade Kauri – City of Auckland Walk ☀ Easy 🚶 1 hour

✳ A stroll along the Waitakere Stream, overhung with tree ferns and nikau palms, leads to two massive kauri trees set in a fine area of native bush.

➤ The track begins at the end of Falls Road, off Te Henga Road between Scenic Drive and Bethells Beach/Te Henga (drive right through the golf course).

The walk begins by crossing the swing bridge below the car park and initially follows the Waitakere Stream, which at this point flows gently through jungle-like vegetation thick with ferns and palms. The Cascades themselves, accessed by a side track, are difficult to see as they are tucked away in a narrow cleft in the rock. The highlight of the walk is two giant kauri which somehow survived early milling of the area. Also keep an eye out for sulphur-crested cockatoos, which have established a colony in the large kauri on the ridge above the stream. You will hear these noisy birds before you see them. From the large kauri the loop track then returns to the car park.

8 Waitakere Dam Easy 🚶 1 hour return

✳ The dam sits on top of a high bluff overlooking the Waitakere Valley, giving excellent views over the ranges.

➤ On Scenic Drive, 7 km north of the intersection with Piha Road.

Built between 1905 and 1910, this was the first reservoir constructed in the Waitakere Ranges to replace the city's water supply at Western Springs. The area around the dam formed the nucleus of Waitakere Ranges Regional Park, which now covers over 17,000 hectares on the fringe of New Zealand's largest city. To assist in the construction of the dam, which at the time was in an isolated part of Auckland, a small tramway was built to bring materials to the site; this still operates. For those wanting a longer walk, there is a track along the tramway as far as the tunnel.

The dam itself is built across the Waitakere River on top of a high bluff and therefore has extensive views over the bush and the valley far below. While the access to the dam is on a sealed roadway, the drop down to the dam is steep, and it is a solid climb back to the car park. On the way back up take a break and visit the large kauri 2 minutes off the main track.

9 Fairy Falls   Medium 🚶 1½ hours return

* A series of attractive cascades with a final drop of 15 metres.

➤ On Scenic Drive, 4.7 km north of the Piha Road intersection. The car park is
opposite the beginning of the track.

These falls are set in very attractive bush with large kauri and rimu along
the way, while Stoney Creek which feeds the falls is a dense jungle of kiekie,
supplejack and nikau. The falls themselves begin as a series of cascades before
a final 15-metre drop into the pool below. The track to the top of the falls is
excellent, but to reach the bottom of the falls is a bit of a scramble down steep
steps, uneven ground and wet rocks, and good footwear is necessary. Think
twice about taking young children all the way to the bottom of the falls as it
is quite an uphill slog on the way back.

10 Whites Beach, Piha   Medium 🚶 1½ hours return

* An isolated west coast beach surrounded by steep bush-clad hills.

➤ The track begins at the very north end of Piha beach.

Accessible only by foot, this beach will appeal to those who enjoy the wild
windswept west coast. The surf is rough and unpredictable even on a good
day, and great care should be taken when swimming. The track to the beach
leads over a headland of regenerating bush of manuka, flax and pohutukawa
with views over both Whites Beach and Piha.

11 Kitekite Falls   Easy 🚶 1 hour return

* The Glen Esk stream tumbles down a series of cascades into a pleasant bush-
lined swimming hole.

➤ At the bottom of the hill to Piha turn immediately right into Glen Esk Road. The
track begins from the car park at the end of this road.

This is the quintessential Waitakere walk. From the car park the broad track
follows the picturesque Glen Esk stream through luxuriant bush steadily
uphill to the falls. The three cascades that make up Kitekite Falls are best

seen from the viewpoint above the valley just before the end of the track. The track also offers views back down the valley over the tops of regenerating kauri. The lower falls drop into a small pool suitable for swimming, and the broad rocky area right by the falls is a good, if lumpy, spot for a picnic. The name of the falls is not so pleasant, however: it commemorates an intertribal massacre of Maori visiting from South Kaipara.

12 Nikau Grove, Piha Easy � 20 minutes return

* ✳ A substantial grove of mature nikau along the Wekatahi Stream.
* ➤ The track begins at the car park at the end of Garden Road, Piha.

The nikau (*Rhopalostylis sapida*) is New Zealand's only member of the palm family and the southernmost palm in the world. Growing to a height of 10 metres, the palm is easily recognised by its upright fronds and distinctive trunk marked by scars from old fronds. Young nikau fronds have a more weeping habit than the mature tree, and give the New Zealand bush a distinctive tropical look. The heart of the palm at the base of the fronds is edible; it was known to early settlers as millionaire's salad as acquiring this food meant the destruction of the entire tree. The bush along this walk flanking the Wekatahi Stream is predominantly nikau, from seedlings through to tall mature plants. When you reach the stream crossing return the way you came.

13 Tasman Lookout Easy (with some steps)

* ✳ Several lookout points offer dramatic coastal views over one of West Auckland's most popular beaches.
* ➤ At the bottom of the hill to Piha turn hard left into Beach Valley Road then, just before the beach, take the left fork into Marine Parade. The track begins at the car park at the end of the road.
* � First lookout: 20 minutes return

  Second lookout: 30 minutes return

  Shore walk (low tide only): 50 minutes return

This coastline is famous for its dramatic seascape. The wilder the weather, the more spectacular the experience along this walk.

The first part of the track leads to a lookout high above Piha with excellent views along the beach to Lion Rock, and north along the coast. It is also the very best spot for watching brave surfers tackle the wild waves of Piha below. From this lookout the track branches to the left, leading to the second lookout above The Gap, a narrow sandy strip between the mainland and Taitomo Island (Camel Rock). Here in rough weather the sea pounds through the rocky gap, though the beach below is surprisingly sheltered. Taitomo Island itself is privately owned Maori land and the land beyond the beach is also privately owned. To reach the beach below it is a bit of a scramble down the bank, especially at the very bottom near the beach. From the beach you can return to Piha along the rocky shore, but only at low tide. This coastline is notorious for rogue waves that wash people off the rocks, often to their death, so don't walk back along the shore if the waves look dicey. Note, too, that dogs are banned from this part of the beach, on account of nesting little blue penguins.

14 Te Ahua Point   Easy   🚶   40 minutes return

* Dramatic sea cliffs dropping hundreds of metres into the wild Tasman Sea combine with spectacular coastal views.

➤ The track begins at the end of Te Ahu Ahu Road/Log Race Road, which turns left off Piha Road just before the road descends into Piha.

Situated between Karekare and Piha beaches, Te Ahua Point is a superb lookout atop towering volcanic cliffs that drop hundreds of metres into a wild sea. To the south the view is along the coast to the dangerous bar that marks the entrance to the Manukau Harbour. On 7 February 1863 the HMS *Orpheus* struck the Manukau bar while trying to enter the harbour. Of the 259 men aboard only 70 survived; this is still New Zealand's worst maritime disaster. Jutting out to sea far to the south is Mt Karioi near Raglan, while to the north is Piha beach and the Muriwai Coast.

The track is well formed and well marked. The grassy knoll at the turnaround point is a good place for a break, though this area is exposed to strong westerly winds. For those wanting a longer walk the track continues downhill to Karekare beach.

15 Whatipu Caves   Easy 🚶 30 minutes return

✳ Several large sea caves huddle behind sand dunes.

➤ Take the road through Titirangi to Huia on the northern side of the Manukau Harbour. From Huia the road to Whatipu is narrow, winding and unsealed. The track starts from the northern side of the car park.

The walk begins on the same track as the Gibbons track (which leads inland), but then branches off to the left and skirts the bottom of the cliff face leading to several large sea caves and a small camping area. Shaped by years of wave action, the caves are now a considerable distance from the sea as the marshy area between the cliffs has built up since 1940. The largest of the caves was once used for dances, though sand has now raised the floor level of the cave by 5 metres. Although the caves are substantial, torches are not necessary. The wetland between the caves and the beach is now an important habitat for waterbirds which can be viewed from the dunes in front of the caves. Do not try to cross the wetlands. Not only will you disturb the birds, the vegetation is also surprisingly dense and the water is deeper than it looks. Return to the car park to get down to the beach.

16 Ninepin Rock and Paratutae   Easy 🚶 1¼ hours

✳ The northern head of the Manukau Harbour is one of the wildest and most scenically dramatic areas of the West Coast.

➤ Start as for the Whatipu Caves walk, but take the track over the bridge from the car park.

The first part of the walk is through dune vegetation to the beach, which leads to Ninepin Rock, the rock with the lighthouse, and to Paratutae, the much larger island to the left. Over the past few years the shoreline in this area has changed dramatically, with powerful westerly storms and strong winds moving huge amounts of sand from season to season. Even on a moderately good day, wild surf pounds the shoreline (swimming is not recommended!), and salt-laden winds whip up the black sand along this exposed coast. However, it is its very wildness that makes this area so appealing. Here, only an hour's drive from downtown Auckland, you can walk along a windswept beach that feels a million miles away from civilisation. On the harbour side of

Paratutae lie a few weathered beams, all that remains of the wharf from where kauri was shipped in vast quantities to Onehunga. A tramline ran from the wharf to Pararaha Valley to the north, though very little of the tramline now remains as the sand and swamp have covered it.

17 Historic Parnell   Easy 🚶 1 hour

> ✳ Historic buildings and hidden parks.

> ➤ Begin the walk on the corner of Parnell Road and St Stephens Ave – a local map will come in handy.

Start at St Mary's in Holy Trinity Cathedral on Parnell Road. Built entirely of timber between 1884 and 1897 by Benjamin Mountfort in the Gothic style, St Mary's has been described as 'one of the finest of all wooden churches in New Zealand'. Originally on the other side of the road, the church was moved to its present site in 1982.

Then walk down St Stephens Ave to number 8, Bishopscourt. Designed by Frederick Thatcher and built between 1861 and 1863, these beautiful wooden buildings are grouped around a central courtyard. Originally built for Bishop Selwyn, Bishopscourt is still the residence of the Anglican Bishop of Auckland and, as such, is not open to the public.

Continue to the very end of tree-lined St Stephens Ave and go down the steps towards the waterfront. Halfway down, just before the bridge over Tamaki Drive, turn left. This path takes you by the Parnell Baths. Originally a tidal swimming pool enclosed by a rock wall, the Parnell Baths is Auckland's only saltwater pool. The building was awarded a Gold Medal in 1958 by the New Zealand Institute of Architects and still features a stylish stone-and-glass mosaic that graces the front of the building.

Continue along the edge of Judges Bay. On the left on a small rise is the historic St Stephen's Chapel. This picturesque small chapel was built for the signing of the Constitution of the Anglican Church of New Zealand in June 1857. Designed by Fredrick Thatcher, the wooden building was used as Bishop Selwyn's semi-private chapel and today functions as a local church.

From Judges Bay take the steps up the hill through Sir Dove-Myer Robinson Park to the lookout over the sea and the city. From here turn around and walk through the Parnell Rose Gardens, famous for their spectacular display of roses in the summer.

Exit left from the gardens and continue walking up Gladstone Road for about 500 metres, then turn right into Alberon Street, and right again into Alberon Place. At the end of this short street take the flight of steps straight ahead that leads down through dense nikau bush to Alberon Reserve. This lovely park edged with palm trees is almost unknown to anyone other than locals, and is a surprise haven in the middle of Parnell. Take the path out of the park to the right, climb up to St Georges Bay Road, and turn right then left into Scarborough Reserve, another pretty park hidden in the small valley below Parnell Road. Take the exit to the right out of this park which leads up to Parnell Road itself. Turn left back up Parnell Road to return to St Mary's.

On the left at 350 Parnell Road is Hulme Court. Built in 1843 in the Regency style, this is reputed to be Auckland's oldest building on its original site. Later purchased by Colonel Hulme, after whom it is named, it was used as Government House during the 1850s and was also at one time the home of Bishop Selwyn. The original bluestone walls have since been plastered over, but the hipped slate roof is original.

18 Mt Eden/Maungawhau   Medium 🚶 1 hour

✱ An extinct volcano with a distinct crater and great views over Auckland city.

➤ Mt Eden Road, Mt Eden.

One of the most popular viewpoints in Auckland, Mt Eden, or Maungawhau (mountain of the whau tree), is a perfectly formed cone with a very distinctive crater. Apihai Te Kawau included Mangawhau in the 3000 acres he gifted to the Crown to establish the settlement of Auckland. Like so many of Auckland's volcanoes, the evidence of terraces, house sites and kumara pits is very clear. The top becomes very crowded with cars and tour buses at times, so walking up is a more pleasant option than driving as the pathways avoid the road for the most part. While you are in the area, considering visiting Eden Gardens at 24 Omana Road, on the eastern slopes of Mt Eden. This botanical gem was established in 1964 in a former quarry and the gardens are reputed to have the broadest collection of camellias in Australasia, as well as an extensive collection of subtropical vireya rhododendrons, clivias and hibiscus.

19 Cornwall Park and One Tree Hill Domain/Maungakiekie

Easy   🏃   1½ hours

Auckland and
Hauraki Gulf

✳ Old trees, an historic building, and the best views in Auckland from the top of One Tree Hill.

➤ The main entrance to the park is off Green Lane West, Greenlane.

The heart of these two adjacent parks is the extinct volcano of One Tree Hill, its volcanic nature evidenced by the very distinctive crater to the west of the summit. Known as Maungakiekie (mountain of the kiekie, a native vine), the area was home to a substantial Maori population supported by the rich volcanic soil. Terraces, kumara pits and house sites cover the higher slopes of the hill. The tree after which One Tree Hill is named has a turbulent past. Originally, a totara tree (Te Totara I Ahua; the totara that stands alone) stood on the summit. This was cut down in the 19th century by a settler for firewood. A number of pine trees were planted, of which one survived, giving the summit its distinctive look through most of the 20th century. This tree in turn was fatally damaged by a Maori protester and was eventually felled in 2001. To date a replacement has not been decided on.

Sir John Logan Campbell, who named the area One Tree Hill after the totara tree and donated the park to Auckland city in 1901, is buried on the summit next to the obelisk.

Cornwall Park is noted for its mature trees including the avenue of oaks and the olive grove situated above the picturesque cricket ground. Acacia Cottage, Auckland's oldest surviving building, was moved to the park in 1920. Built in 1841, it was originally situated in Shortland Street in the city where it was occupied by John Logan Campbell and his business partner, William Brown. Now restored, the house contains period furniture, and is open to the public.

The park is laced with paths. Being both gardens and a working farm, it is open and impossible to get lost in. There is a long walk around the perimeter of the park that takes about an hour, and this can be combined with an inner loop that takes in the summit.

20 Musick Point   Easy   🚶 20 minutes return

* Excellent views over Browns Island and the entrance to the Waitemata Harbour.

➤ The entrance to the point is through the Howick Golf Club, Musick Point Road, Bucklands Beach.

The name is not a spelling mistake but the surname of pioneer flying boat aviator Captain Edwin Musick, who was lost with his crew in the Pacific in January 1938. Originally a Maori pa site, the point has wide views over the Hauraki Gulf with the centrepiece being the deco-style heritage building Musick Point Air Radio Station. Opened in 1942 and operated by the Post Office, this building provided radio contact for ships and aircraft. It is still in use today providing cellular services for Telecom. Beyond the radio station the track, which is quite rough in places, winds around the point and a steep flight of steps leads down the cliff for those keen on further exploring the rocky shoreline. There are excellent views of the inner Gulf islands and especially the volcanic cone of Browns Island, which lies just offshore.

21 Duder Regional Park   Medium   🚶 1½ hours

* Magnificent views of the Coromandel Peninsula, Firth of Thames and the islands of the inner Gulf, and an historic landing site of the waka Tainui.

➤ From SH1 travel towards Whitford and on to Maraetai, then follow the coast south to Umupuia Beach. From the southern end of Umupuia Beach turn right into North Road. The entrance to the park is on the right a short distance down this road.

Duder Regional Park occupies the Whakakaiwhara Peninsula and is currently almost entirely farmed with just a few tiny patches of bush. Around AD 1300 the waka Tainui anchored at very end of the peninsula while sheltering from a storm, and is remembered in the place name Te Tauranga o Tainui. Whakakaiwhara pa was strategically located at the very tip of the peninsula, and terraces, kumara pits and defensive ditches are still visible today. The Duder family purchased the land in 1866, and continued to farm it up to 1994 when it was sold to the Auckland Regional Council for a park.

The farm loop walk is best undertaken anticlockwise following the south coast of the peninsula. This gives a comfortable steady hill climb to the trig point, which has grand views over the Firth of Thames, the Gulf islands of Waiheke, Ponui, Browns and Rangitoto, and to the east the blue-tinged Coromandel Peninsula. A further track leads out to the point; this will add another 50 minutes.

22 Tawhitokino Bay   Easy 人 1 hour return

✳ A beautiful stretch of beach fringed by pohutukawa and safe for swimming at all tides.

➤ From Kawakawa Bay, follow the coast road for 4 km east to Waiti Bay to the car park at the very end of the road. The track leaves the car park from the right.

This little-known bay is a gem on the Firth of Thames coast. Its long sandy beach, fringed by pohutukawa trees, is pleasantly empty even on a hot summer's day. It is safe for swimming at all tides and has an uninterrupted view of the Coromandel Peninsula. The track undulates through regenerating bush and passes through the equally attractive Tuturau Bay.

23 Mangere Mountain   Easy 人 1 hour

✳ Next to Rangitoto, this is Auckland's largest and most original volcanic cone.

➤ Main entrance at the end of Domain Road, off Coronation Road, Mangere Bridge.

One of the largest and least modified of Auckland's 50 volcanic cones, Mangere Mountain is a quiet haven compared with the better-known volcanoes. The rich volcanic soils sustained a large Maori population in pre-European times, growing kumara and taro, with easy access to seafood in the Manukau Harbour. Maori land boundaries indicated by low stone walls fan out from the base of the mountain, and kumara pits and house sites are clearly visible inside the crater. There are excellent views out over the Manukau Harbour from the top. The track follows the rim of the crater, but as the whole park is open grass, you can just stroll anywhere. The Visitor Centre on Coronation Road is an alternative starting point, though the displays are mainly geared to schoolchildren.

24 Auckland Botanic Gardens
Easy   𝄠   1 hour (or more)

✳ A large open garden combining formal gardens with more open park-like grounds and a short bush walk through adjoining Totara Park.

➤ Hill Road, Manurewa, signposted off the Southern Motorway.

Opened in 1982 on 64 hectares in Manurewa, the gardens may lack old-world garden charm but this is more than made up for by the fascinating range of plants not possible in confined older city gardens. The gardens are ideal for a long ramble through a diverse array of over 10,000 plants in 24 collections ranging from formal flower beds (the dahlias are incredible) and rose gardens through to the more exotic South African collection. It is worth taking the time to stroll through Totara Park (just north of and adjoining the gardens) as this is a fine remnant of mature totara bush, rare in the Auckland area. Entrance to the gardens is free and there is an excellent café in the smart new Visitor Centre.

25 Awhitu Regional Park   Easy   𝄠   1 hour

✳ An historic homestead sits in a pleasant farm park on the shores of the Manukau Harbour.

➤ From Waiuku drive north along the Awhitu Peninsula to Matakawau; 2 km past Matakawau turn right into Brook Road, which leads to the park.

Nestled on the sheltered eastern side of the Awhitu Peninsula on the Manukau Harbour, this attractive park is a lovely combination of natural and human history. At the heart of the park is the 19th-century Brook Homestead, typical of the comfortable farm villas of the day and set among fine old trees on a rise above the beach. Just in front of the homestead is a small roughly built cottage which initially housed the family until sufficient money was available to build a more substantial home.

The area is very tidal and is honestly more attractive closer to high tide, though the tidal flats do provide an important feeding ground for birds. Within the park are substantial wetlands, home to shy and elusive fernbirds, bitterns and banded rails.

26 Hunua Falls   Easy 𐀪 20 minutes

✳ An impressive 28-metre waterfall and a popular swimming hole.

➤ From Hunua Village drive north and then turn right into White Road. After 1 km, turn right into Falls Road; the car park is another 2 km.

Especially impressive after heavy rain, these 28-metre falls flow over hard basalt rock, the rim of an ancient volcano. There is a good picnic ground here and the huge pool at the base of the falls is a popular swimming spot. Two short walks on either side of the pool lead to lookout points over it.

27 Waiheke: Stony Batter   Easy 𐀪 1 hour

✳ Excellent views of the Hauraki Gulf from this extensive and well preserved Second World War fortification.

➤ 6 km from Onetangi at the end of Man O'War Bay Road.

Stony Batter is at the less-developed eastern end of Waiheke Island and is not easy to get to. While the batter is only a 20-minute walk from the end of the road, getting that far can be tricky as there is no public transport. Cars and bikes can be hired near the ferry wharf. If you are planning to cycle, the road beyond Onetangi is very hilly, with the last 6 km gravel.

One of the most impressive remains of New Zealand's coastal defence system, this complex was begun in 1942 to protect the northern approaches to Auckland from the Japanese. In reality the batter was not completed until 1948, well after the war was over, and the guns were never fired in defence. While very little exists above ground, the underground rooms are largely intact and surprisingly fresh in appearance. The walk is along a gravel road past olive groves, grape vines, small patches of bush and distinctive boulders from which the batter takes its name. The open and lofty location gives excellent views over the Gulf, and a track leads down to Hooks Bay for those wanting a longer walk.

There is a small charge for access to the underground tunnels to support the maintenance of the area.

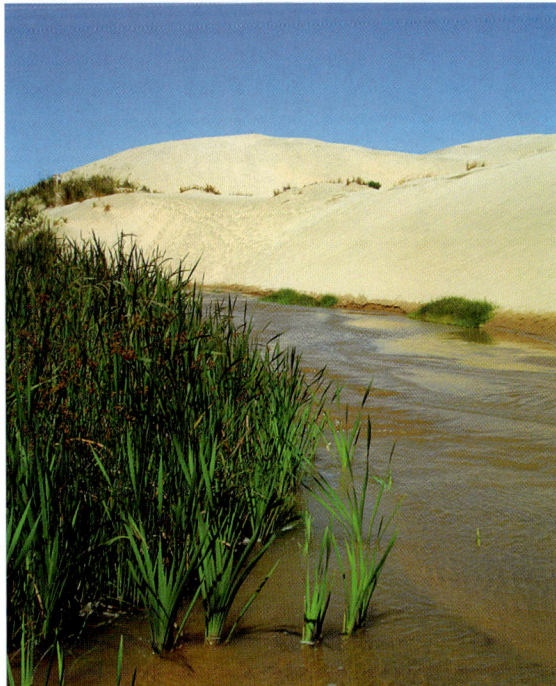

Above Te Werahi Beach, Cape Reinga. Thousands of visitors flock to the cape to witness the dramatic clash of the Tasman Sea and the Pacific Ocean. From the same car park, very few venture to beautiful Te Werahi Beach, just 45 minutes away along a spectacular clifftop walk.

Left Te Paki Sand Hills. The shallow Te Paki Stream, which leads down to the northern end of Ninety Mile Beach, skirts the golden sand hills popular for both walking and 'sandboarding'.

St Paul's Rock, Whangaroa Harbour. The harbour's fiord-like beauty is revealed after a short but steep ascent up this old volcanic plug and former Maori pa site.

Left Waitangi Mangrove. Mangroves are common in the tidal harbours in the North Island, but it is only in Northland that they reach the height of small trees. Low tide is the best time to see the peculiar aerial roots of this highly adaptable tree.

Below Smugglers Bay, Whangarei Heads. Not just a fanciful name, but a real smugglers' hideout. Here in the 19th century they brought barrels of whisky ashore at night and hid them in the sand dunes to avoid paying duty at the Whangarei wharves.

Tane Mahuta, Waipoua Forest. The majestic 'Lord of the Forest' is New Zealand's largest kauri. Nearby in the same forest are three excellent short walks to other impressive kauri trees and groves.

Left Wenderholm Regional Park, Auckland. This impressive pou guards the entrance to a walk up through mature bush to a lookout over the Hauraki Gulf. The walk begins at pohutukawa-fringed Wenderholm Beach, lined with excellent picnic spots.

Below Whatipu, Auckland. Arriving at wild and windswept Whatipu it is hard to believe that a city of over a million people is just an hour away. A small lighthouse atop Ninepin Rock guides ships over the treacherous Manukau bar, the site of New Zealand's worst maritime disaster.

Left One Tree Hill, Auckland. The land for the park (in Maori, Maungakiekie) was gifted to the city in 1901 by mayor John Logan Campbell, known as 'The Father of Auckland'. Actually two parks, Cornwall Park and One Tree Hill Domain, this iconic landmark is both a public park and a working farm.

Below Kawau Island. The stark outline of the pumphouse chimney (left) is all that remains of a short-lived copper mine on the island. Mansion House (right) was the home of Governor George Grey, who planted it with exotic trees such as these Chilean wine palms.

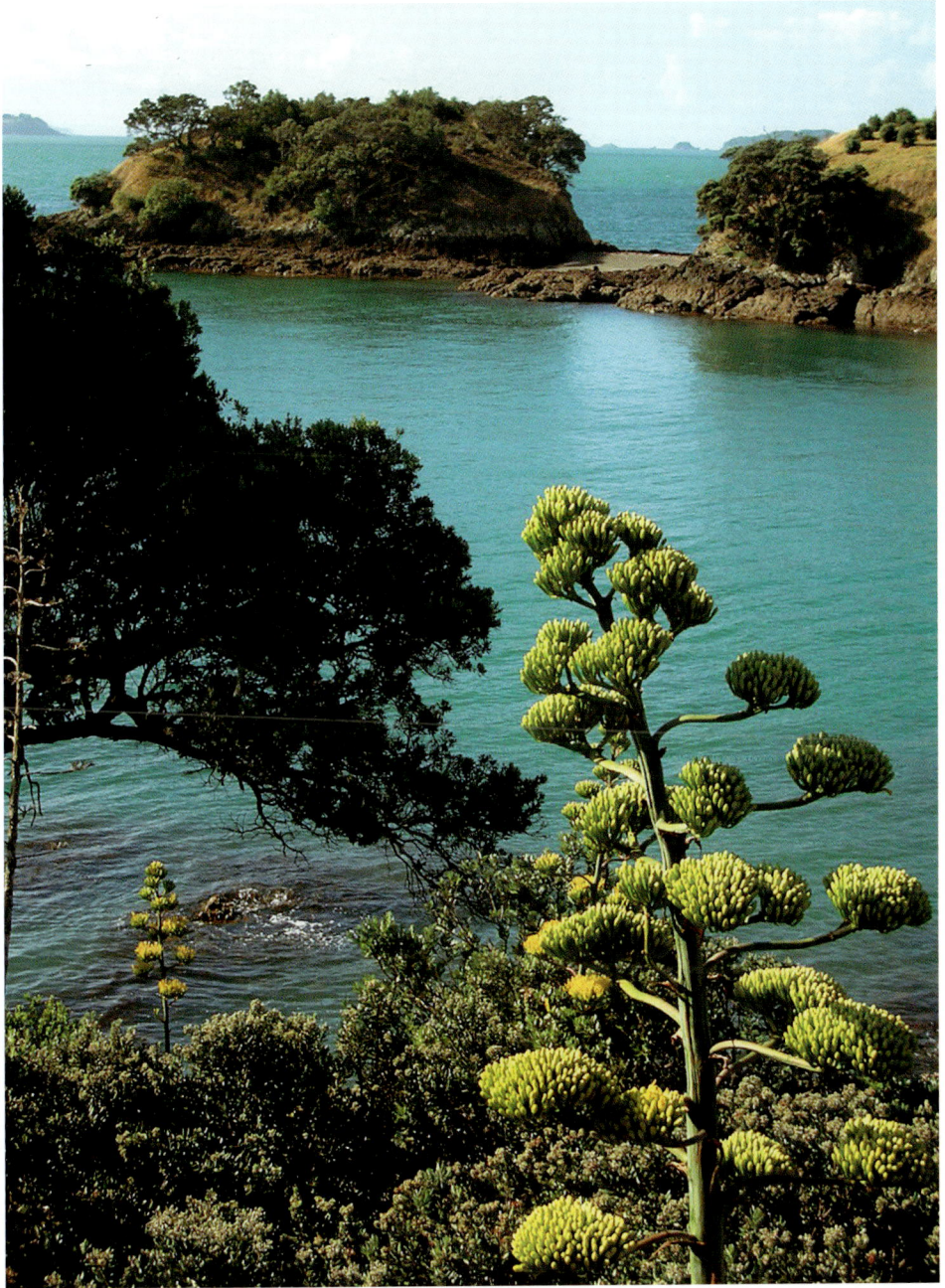

Matietie Historic Reserve, Waiheke Island. Old pa sites and magnificent views of the Hauraki Gulf make this walk one of the most popular on Waiheke, which is easily accessible by ferry from Auckland.

Above Opoutere Beach, Coromandel.
Even at the height of summer this
wide sweep of sand is hardly crowded.
Opoutere is also an important nesting
area for wading birds such as the New
Zealand dotterel.

Right Te Koutu Lake, Cambridge.
In a sheltered basin in the heart of
Cambridge this tranquil haven of
mature trees and waterlily-covered lake
lies just off busy State Highway 1.

28 Waiheke: School Loop Track, Whakanewha Regional Park Easy 🚶 30 minutes

* A rare patch of native bush in this relatively new regional park.

➤ On Gordons Road, off O'Brien Road, Rocky Bay.

Located on the southern side of the island, this short track leads up from the beach to a lookout point with views over Whakanewha or Rocky Bay, and back towards Auckland city. From the lookout the track passes through regenerating and mature bush fragments to an old pa site, with kumara pits clearly visible. From here the track leads down to Poukaraka flats with its old pohutukawa trees and broad grassy area ideal for picnics. New Zealand dotterels nest here during the summer. It is best to time your visit to coincide with high tide when the bay is at its most attractive.

29 Waiheke: Matietie Historic Reserve
Medium 🚶 1 hour 10 minutes

* Coastal views of Auckland and the Gulf and a close-up peek at some rather amazing houses.

➤ The walk begins and ends from Matiatia, the main Waiheke wharf. The start of the walk is not marked as such; access is via the shoreline beyond the Matietie Reserve sign to the left of the car park.

Ideal for those who are going to Waiheke for the day on the ferry and do not want to venture too far afield on the island, the walk follows the coast around to Cable Bay and then returns inland to Matiatia. The walk begins to the north of the car park by the wharf; if the tide is right in, the first part of the walk is a scramble over rocks and tree roots for about 100 metres. This is by far the most difficult part of the track. From the small bay just beyond the wharf the walk then follows the markers around the coast. Here the track winds its way through open grass, and links rocky headlands with small gravel beaches easily accessed by short side tracks. The wide views include downtown Auckland and the islands of the inner Gulf: Rangitoto, Motutapu, Motuihe, The Noises, Tiritiri Matangi and, in the far distance, Little Barrier. On the headland the terraces of an old pa site are clearly visible (in pre-European times Waiheke was home to around 1000 Maori), and old pohutukawa cling to rocky cliffs. As an extra bonus, this track passes close to some of Waiheke's most expensive houses and parts of the walk are like strolling through the pages of a design magazine.

At Cable Bay, easily identified by the triangular cable sign, turn right uphill until you hit the road, then turn left and continue down the road to the track which leads off to the right just past the locked road gate. This takes you back to Matiatia. For those wanting a longer walk, from Cable Bay continue along the steep track uphill and on to Owhanake Bay, then turn inland where the track takes you back to the road leading to the wharf. This longer walk will take about 2 hours.

30 Kawau Island Easy 🚶 1½ hours return

* In addition to Governor Grey's Mansion House there are the romantic ruins of an old copper mine.

➤ Two companies run ferries to the island: 360 Discovery (www.360discovery.co.nz, phone 0800 360 3472), and Ruebens Water Taxi (www.ruebens.co.nz, phone 0800 111 616)

The original house on Kawau Island was built in 1845 for the manager of the nearby copper mine. In 1862 George Grey (Premier of New Zealand 1877–79) purchased Kawau Island for 3500 pounds, and over the years greatly expanded the house, planted exotic trees, and stocked the island with an array of animals including monkeys, zebras, kookaburras and wallabies. Many of the trees remain, and there is still a colony of kookaburras on the mainland. The Parma wallaby from Australia is now extinct in that country, and wallabies from Kawau (where they are a pest) have been shipped home.

Copper mining began on the island as early as 1844. While the 20-metre chimney of the engine room at the copper mine is all that remains, the mine shafts actually went deep under the sea below the engine room. The rocks around the chimney are a very distinct green, the colour of copper in its natural form.

31 Great Barrier Island: Kaitoke Hot Springs

Easy   人   2 hours return

* Water from a natural hot spring merges with the cooler Kaitoke Stream.

➤ For ferry and flight options to Great Barrier Island (www.thebarrier.co.nz).

Just 5 km from Whangaparapara on Whangaparapara Road at a fork in the Kaitoke Stream, a natural hot spring wells up from subterranean depths to mingle with the cooler waters of the stream. It is a pleasant 2-hour return walk to the springs, mainly through regenerating bush. The stream water is quite shallow and it is not easy to get a good warm soak despite all attempts to dam the stream.

Auckland and Hauraki Gulf

32 Great Barrier Island: Windy Canyon

Medium   人   45 minutes return

* A rugged volcanic canyon high on Mt Hobson.

➤ For ferry and flight options to Great Barrier Island (www.thebarrier.co.nz).
The walk is signposted from the summit of Whangapoua Hill on Aotea Road.

The rugged outcrops of Windy Canyon are testament to the volcanic origins of Mt Hobson/Hirakimata, and the track picks its way through a rugged dramatic canyon (though steps make the going quite easy). Keep an eye out for the glass-like obsidian embedded in the rocky walls and the Great Barrier tea-tree and daisy, both found only on the island.

33 Rangitoto Island: McKenzie Bay and Lighthouse

Easy   人   2 hours return

* An historic lighthouse sits just off Rangitoto's only sandy beach.

➤ Fullers runs a regular ferry to the island (www.fullers.co.nz, phone 09 367 9111) but take care not to miss your ferry back as there is no overnight accommodation on the island and alternative transport to the mainland is expensive. The walk begins from the wharf.

The largest and youngest of Auckland's volcanoes, Rangitoto erupted from the sea about 600–700 years ago and was last active only 350 years ago. The island has unusual plant life adapted to the raw lava environment, and in recent years has been cleared of exotic pests such as possums and the brush-tailed wallaby. Many of the roads and stone walls and the swimming pool were built by prison labour in the 1920s and '30s, and still remain.

From the wharf the coastal track leads through pohutukawa forest to Rangitoto's only sandy beach. The concrete lighthouse was first built in 1882, but it took over 20 years to sort out a dispute between the Auckland Harbour Board and the Marine Department before the lighthouse finally began operation in 1905. The track passes several of Rangitoto's famous baches (small holiday houses). In the 1920s and '30s Aucklanders built baches on public land at Rangitoto Wharf, Islington Bay and McKenzie Bay. Most have now been removed, but around 30 baches have been kept as examples of the innovative do-it-yourself beach culture of the period.

34 Rangitoto Summit   Medium ⅄ 2 hours return

✳ A magnificent vista not only of the island but also of the entire Hauraki Gulf, Waitemata Harbour and Auckland city.

➤ Fullers runs a regular ferry to the island (www.fullers.co.nz, phone 09 367 9111) but take care not to miss your ferry back as there is no overnight accommodation on the island and alternative transport to the mainland is expensive. The walk begins from the wharf.

The walk to the summit (259 metres) is a steady climb on a well-formed path and leads to a magnificent view over Auckland and the Hauraki Gulf. The crater and summit are actually covered in reasonably large trees as the original volcanic eruptions that created the cone occurred in the very early stages of the island's creation and the last eruptions were much further down the western slope. A side track just below the summit (20 minutes return) leads to extensive lava caves, some collapsed and some intact. It is possible to scramble through the caves; a torch is useful.

The flora of Rangitoto have had to adapt to a harsh environment of barren, dry lava fields. One tree that manages is the pohutukawa, and the island is home to the largest pohutukawa forest in the world (the honey of which is now internationally renowned for its medicinal properties). Another plant is the fascinating kidney fern. Usually glossy, wet and very fragile-looking, this fern shrivels up like a very dry leaf in hot weather, returning to normal only when there is sufficient moisture.

✳ New Zealand's most accessible bird sanctuary, preserving some of the country's most endangered species.

➤ 360 Discovery run ferries from both downtown Auckland, Whangaparaoa Peninsula, and Sandspit, near Warkworth (www.360discovery.co.nz, phone 0800 360 3472 or 09 424 5510).

Tiritiri Matangi is both an inspirational conservation story and the country's most accessible island bird sanctuary, home to some of New Zealand's rarest birds.

Stripped of its native bush, Tiritiri was farmed from 1850 to 1970, with only a few coastal remnants remaining on this small, relatively flat island of only 230 hectares. In a bold move the Department of Conservation embarked on a programme not only to replant the island, but also to develop it as an open sanctuary with easy access for the public. Equally importantly, it was decided to involve the public in tree planting, and there is hardly an Auckland schoolchild who wasn't involved in the massive operation to plant over a quarter of a million trees between 1984 and 1994. The result has been an overwhelming success and led not only to a haven for endangered birds but also to this island being used as a model for many other such reserves around the country.

Once the predators were removed and some cover established, recovery of birdlife was spectacular. Over 70 species of bird have been sighted on the island, of which 11 were relocated here. The birds include takahe, hihi (stitchbird), little spotted kiwi, brown teal, kokako, saddleback, bellbird and kakariki (New Zealand parakeet), many of which are very common on the island, especially around the bird-feeding stations.

The island has a maze of tracks of varied lengths. The walk from the wharf to the lighthouse will take about 50 minutes return, while a walk around the island can take up to 3 hours. The island terrain is rolling, and none of the tracks is difficult. Recommended, and costing only a few dollars more, is the short guided walk from the wharf to the historic lighthouse given by the ranger when arriving on the island. Hobbs Bay, a 5-minute walk from the wharf, is the best swimming beach.

Auckland and Hauraki Gulf

Coromandel

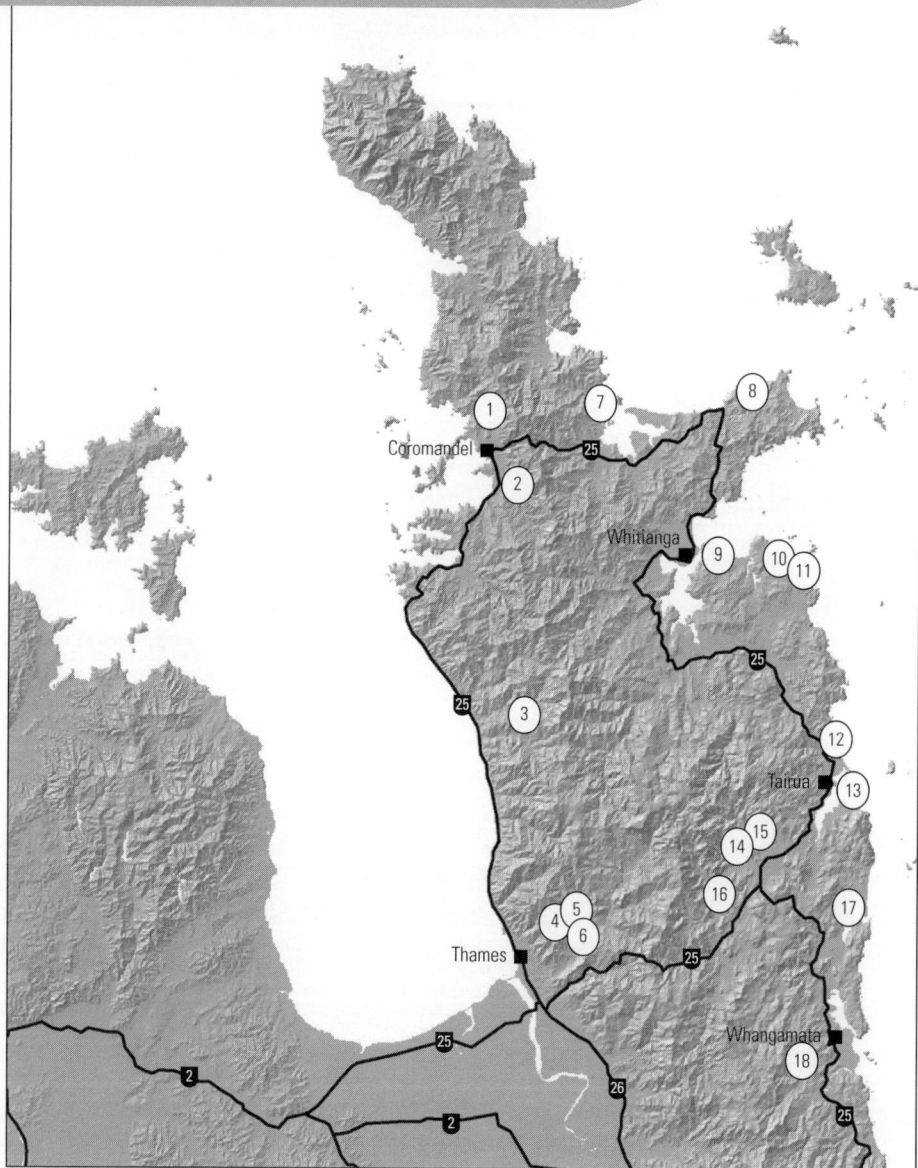

Coromandel

Whitianga

Tairua

Thames

Whangamata

54

1 Tokatea/Lucas Lookout Medium ⅄ 20 minutes return

* ✳ Great view over Coromandel Harbour and Kennedy Bay.

* ➤ From Coromandel town take Driving Creek Road towards Kennedy Bay. The walk begins 4 km up this road at the summit.

From this hill, Coromandel town and harbour and small offshore islands are spread below, while across the Firth of Thames lie the Hunua Ranges and the islands of the Hauraki Gulf. To the west is Kennedy Bay, the Kuaotunu Peninsula and, offshore, the Mercury Islands. There is a directional table on the top which is handy in locating all the key geographical features.

The track starts at the concrete steps, but don't try this walk just wearing shorts and a T-shirt. Despite the good view the track is not well maintained, and at the time of writing was overgrown with particularly vicious gorse bushes. If you are not wearing long sleeves and long trousers you will be badly scratched.

2 Waiau Kauri Grove and Waterfall Easy ⅄ 20 minutes return

* ✳ A grove of mature kauri including a tree with a double trunk.

* ➤ Just south of Coromandel town turn onto the 309 Road which is narrow, winding and unsealed. The kauri grove is on the left, 8 km from the turn-off.

This small grove of massive old kauri luckily escaped the miller's axe, and this rare patch of mature forest is now accessible by an excellent short track. The boardwalk at one point entirely surrounds the trunk of a kauri so it is possible to touch and feel the texture of the bark. A short loop walk leads to an unusual double-trunked tree, which began life as two seedlings that eventually grew together and fused at the base. A short distance down the road, and just a 2-minute walk from it, are the small but pretty Waiau Falls with a little pool.

Coromandel

3 Square Kauri   Medium   𝄌   20 minutes return

✴ A magnificent kauri that is distinctively square in cross section.

➤ 9 km from Tapu on the Tapu–Coroglen Road.

A short walk leads to this huge kauri, over 41 metres high and estimated to be 1200 years old. Named for the relatively squarish nature of the trunk, the short track is all steps up to the tree. An extra bonus is a great lookout over the ranges and across the valley to Maumaupaki or Camels Back (822 metres).

Kauaeranga Valley

It was timber, not gold, that attracted Europeans to this valley leading deep into the heart of the Coromandel hills behind Thames. From 1871 through to 1928 the magnificent kauri forests were milled virtually to extinction, and while the scars of the forestry era still remain, the bush has reclaimed much of the land, and the old pack tracks and tramlines used to haul logs out of the bush now form part of the extensive track system. The following three tracks are a small taste of what the Kauaeranga Valley has to offer. Take some time to check out the new Visitor Centre, which displays information and photographs of both the natural and the human history of the valley.

4 Kauaeranga Valley: Model Dam/Kahikatea Walk
Easy   𝄌   20 minutes return

✴ A working small-scale wooden kauri dam.

➤ From just south of the Thames shopping centre turn into Kauaeranga Valley Road. The Visitor Centre is 14 km down this road, which for the most part is sealed. The walk begins from the Visitor Centre car park.

Huge wooden dams were used extensively in the Kauaeranga Valley right up until the 1920s, though today only the remains of two dams still exist high in the valley. One dam trip, involving several dams, brought a staggering 28,000 kauri logs down the valley. Using the design of the actual Tarawaere dam, this model is one-third the size of the original. Excellent information boards show exactly how the dam worked.

5 Kauaeranga Valley: Hoffman's Pool and Nature Walk
Easy

* A beautiful sandy swimming hole.

➤ From just south of the Thames shopping centre turn into Kauaeranga Valley Road. The Visitor Centre is 14 km down this road, which for the most part is sealed. The walk begins 1.8 km from the Visitor Centre.

人 Hoffman's Pool: 5 minutes

Nature Walk: 30 minutes

The nature walk rambles through regenerating bush linking a number of points of interest including:

- A view of the Chief's Head, a rocky outcrop that really does look like a head.
- An old stone wall, all that remains of the Thames water supply established in 1874.
- Hoffman's Pool, a popular swimming hole at the point where the Kauaeranga River divides. Deep and clear, there is a rock to jump off, and – even better – part of the pool has a lovely sandy bottom.
- The concrete slab by the pool, all that remains of the Kauaeranga Tramline which crossed the river at this point.

There are two entrances to this walk, which are just 250 metres apart. The first entrance is to the Nature Walk, and the interpretive signs are numbered from this end. However, if you plan to swim go to the second entrance (the car park is on the left), as this is just a short walk to Hoffman's Pool.

6 Kauaeranga Valley: Edward's Lookout
Medium 人 45 minutes return

* A great view deep into the jagged peaks of the Coromandel Range.

➤ From just south of the Thames shopping centre turn into Kauaeranga Valley Road. The Visitor Centre is 14 km down this road, which for the most part is sealed. This walk begins 5.4 km past the Visitor Centre.

A steady uphill walk on an excellent track (all metal, no mud!) leads to a rocky outcrop high above the river. From here there are fantastic views deep

Coromandel

into the ranges with the obviously named Table Mountain to the left, and the equally obviously named Pinnacles to the right. Below, the road slices through the upper reaches of the Kauaeranga Valley, now entirely bush-covered and with no traces visible of the substantial timber industry that once stripped the hills bare of their kauri forests.

7 Opera Point   Easy 🚶 30 minutes return

✳ A bush-covered headland with sea views, an old pa site and a small sandy beach.

➤ At Te Rerenga, on the road from Coromandel to Whitianga, turn off to Whangapoua. The car park is 5 km on the right just before Whangapoua settlement.

A 15-minute walk follows an old tramway through a nikau gully to a small but secluded beach. (You will get your feet wet at high tide.) The flat area behind the beach was the site of Craig's sawmill, established in 1862, while on the headland above is the fortified Ruakawa pa with its defence trenches still clearly visible. It is a bit of a scramble up to the pa, but worth the effort as the outlook over the Whangapoua Harbour to Matarangi is extensive and it is very obvious why this point was chosen as a defended site. There is an unformed but reasonably clear track that returns from the headland back along the ridge to the car park.

8 Otama Beach   Easy 🚶 30 minutes one way along the beach

✳ An undeveloped beach with a dune reserve.

➤ From Kuaotunu take Black Jack Road. Otama Beach is 5 km along this road, which is narrow, unsealed and winding.

For many people Otama is the total Coromandel beach experience. A long stretch of white sand with only a few houses at the southern end, the beach is backed by sand dunes that are now a nature reserve protecting the whole length of the beach from further development. The beach looks out over the Mercury Islands. The best access is from the northern end at the bottom of the Black Jack hill. There is a basic camping ground at Otama (water but no toilets).

Coromandel

9 Shakespeare Cliff and Lonely Bay   Easy

✳ Great views over Mercury Bay, and a small sandy cove.

➤ Located between Cooks Beach and Flaxmill Bay, with tracks leading to the headland from both. From Whitianga township it is possible to cross by ferry and then walk to Flaxmill Bay, which will take around 25 minutes. The track to the lookout point is marked at the far end of the bay.

🚶 Lookout: 5 minutes

Lonely Bay: 20 minutes

Ferry Landing: 1½ hours

After landing at Cooks Beach (and obviously naming it after himself) in November 1769, Lieutenant James Cook observed the transit of Mercury across the face of the sun, and thereby accurately calculated his longitude and latitude position (hence the name Mercury Bay). The headland has extensive views over the bay, and a plaque commemorates Cook's visit and indicates features around the bay. Cook fancied he saw the likeness of an orator reciting Shakespeare outlined in the cliff, and named the area after the bard.

A steep track from the car park leads down to the quiet, pohutukawa-lined Lonely Bay, one of Coromandel's loveliest small beaches, and perfect for swimming. The lower section of the steps, a project of the Japanese Society of Mercury Bay, was designed by sculptor and architect Akio Hizume.

10 Hahei: Cathedral Cove   Medium 🚶 1½ hours return

✳ A stunning sandy cove backed by pohutukawa and divided by a rock arch.

➤ From SH25 take Hot Water Beach Road, Link Road and Hahei Beach Road to Hahei, a distance of 10 km. At the Hahei store turn left into Grange Road and continue 1.5 km to the car park at the end.

This beautiful small beach fringed with pohutukawa trees is the quintessential Coromandel beach, but is becoming a bit crowded in the height of the holiday season. The two parts of the beach are linked by a high-arched sea cave (hence the name Cathedral Cove), and the coastline is now protected as part of the Te-Whanganui-A-Hei Marine Reserve. The beach access is along a well-formed track which takes around 45 minutes each way. There are toilet facilities at the beach itself.

Coromandel

11 Hahei: Te Pare Historic Reserve Easy 30 minutes return

✳ A coastal pa site with great views over Mercury Bay.

➤ The track to the pa site begins at the end of Pa Road, or leads up from the southern end of the beach.

Stronghold of Ngati Hei, who arrived in the area on the waka Arawa in AD 1350, this must be one of the most beautifully situated pa sites in the country. The broad terraces that occupy this rocky headland, with the sea on three sides, have the most magnificent outlook over Mercury Bay and Hahei Beach. Another pa is clearly visible on the hill behind Te Pare, while the rocks below are a popular fishing spot and, of course, Hahei itself is a very safe beach for swimming.

12 Tairua: Paku Peak Medium 30 minutes return

✳ Coastal views from this old pa site.

➤ From the Tairua shopping centre on SH2 turn into Manaia Road, then turn into Paku Drive and follow the road to the car park at the top.

Discovered by Kupe around AD 950, the Coromandel coast has a long history of settlement by Maori, who were originally attracted to the area by the now extinct moa and the abundant seafood. The only known artefact linking Aotearoa to Eastern Polynesia, a shellfish hook, was found on the beach at Tairua. In European times Tairua began life as a timber-milling town, and vast quantities of kauri and other native timber were shipped out from this small port on the Tairua River. Today visitors are attracted by the fine sweep of surf beach that faces out to Slipper and Shoe Islands and, beyond them, The Aldermen Islands. A short rocky scramble leads to the top of the volcanic peak Paku, with dramatic coastal and inland views. Once an island, it is easy to see why this strategic peak was a major fortified pa.

13 Mt Pauanui Hard ⅄ 1½ hours return

* ✹ Great views over Pauanui, Tairua and the rocky coast to the south.
* ➤ The walk is clearly marked from the southern end of Pauanui beach.

The climb to the top of Mt Pauanui (387 metres) is steep, but the track is very good, and the sweat is rewarded by fantastic views north over Pauanui and Tairua, and to the south as far as Mt Maunganui.

Broken Hills

Gold was discovered at Broken Hills in 1893, and a flourishing town existed here through to the 1930s. Today a maze of short walks – three of which follow here – leads to a fascinating array of old mine shafts, battery sites and tunnels. The Tairua River meanders through the valley, now mostly cloaked in regenerating bush. This is a great place to bring children and explore.

14 Broken Hills: Gem of the Boom Creek Easy ⅄ 25 minutes

* ✹ A gloomy cave jail that will appeal immensely to children.
* ➤ Take Morrison Road opposite the Pauanui turn-off on SH25 and after 1 km turn left into Puketui Road. This walk begins 250 metres before the bridge car park.

The highlight of this loop walk through the bush is the old Broken Hills jail, a shady cave dug into the hillside.

15 Broken Hills: Golden Hills Battery Easy ⅄ 30 minutes

* ✹ The fascinating ruins of an old battery.
* ➤ Take Morrison Road opposite the Pauanui turn-off on SH25 and after 1 km turn left into Puketui Road. This walk starts from the bridge car park.

Following the southern bank of the Tairua River, this track leads to the ruins of a battery built in 1899. What remains among the bush is a jumble of arches and concrete walls from the old cyanide tanks that looks more like a monastery than a gold mine battery.

16 Broken Hills: Collins Drive   Medium 𝄇 2 hours

* A 500-metre tunnel.

➤ Take Morrison Road opposite the Pauanui turn-off on SH25 and after 1 km turn
  left into Puketui Valley Road. This walk starts from the car park at the end of the
  road.

On the north bank of the river, several tracks zigzag up the hills following an
old water race and climbing to Collins Drive. The water-race track follows an
old waterway, in places cut deep into the contour of the hill and including a
number of low tunnels.

Much further up the hill is the impressive Collins Drive, a 500-metre
tunnel created not to find gold, but as an access tunnel through steep country.
A torch is necessary for Collins Drive. There are some great lookout points
from this track as well.

17 Opoutere Beach   Easy

* A wide sweep of empty beach and an important wildlife sanctuary.

➤ The turn-off to Opoutere is 10 km north of Whangamata; beach access is a
  further 5 km from the turn-off.

𝄇 Beach: 20 minutes return

Loop walk: 1 hour

One of the few undeveloped beaches on the Coromandel, this gives a taste
of what this coast was like before the baches took over. Access is over a
tidal mangrove-lined stream, and then through dunes. Even in the middle of
summer it is not hard to find a quiet spot on this long sweep of sandy beach.
The loop walk takes you south to the harbour entrance and the Wharekawa
Sandspit Wildlife Refuge. This is an important breeding ground for several
endangered birds, including the New Zealand dotterel, and the nesting
grounds are roped off during the spring and summer. Although the nests are
mere scrapings in the sand, the eggs blend perfectly with the environment
and are easy to miss. Not so easy to miss are the aggressive parent birds who
will make it very clear that you have strayed into their territory. From the end
of the beach follow the harbour shore back to where a track leads through the
trees to the main access track to the beach.

Coromandel

18 Wentworth Falls
Easy   🚶   2 hours

✳ An attractive waterfall deep in the bush.

➤ Wentworth Valley Road is off SH25, 2 km south of Whangamata.

The Wentworth Falls tumble over a 50-metre rocky bluff to a good-sized pool ideal for swimming on a warm summer's afternoon. Once a bustling gold mining settlement and a major access track across the Coromandel to the Maratoto Valley, the track to the falls is now through thick native bush with little remaining of early goldmining activities.

There is a viewing platform overlooking the falls, and a tricky narrow track to the swimming hole at the bottom of the falls. The track continues beyond the platform to a viewpoint at the top of the waterfall.

Coromandel

Waikato and King Country

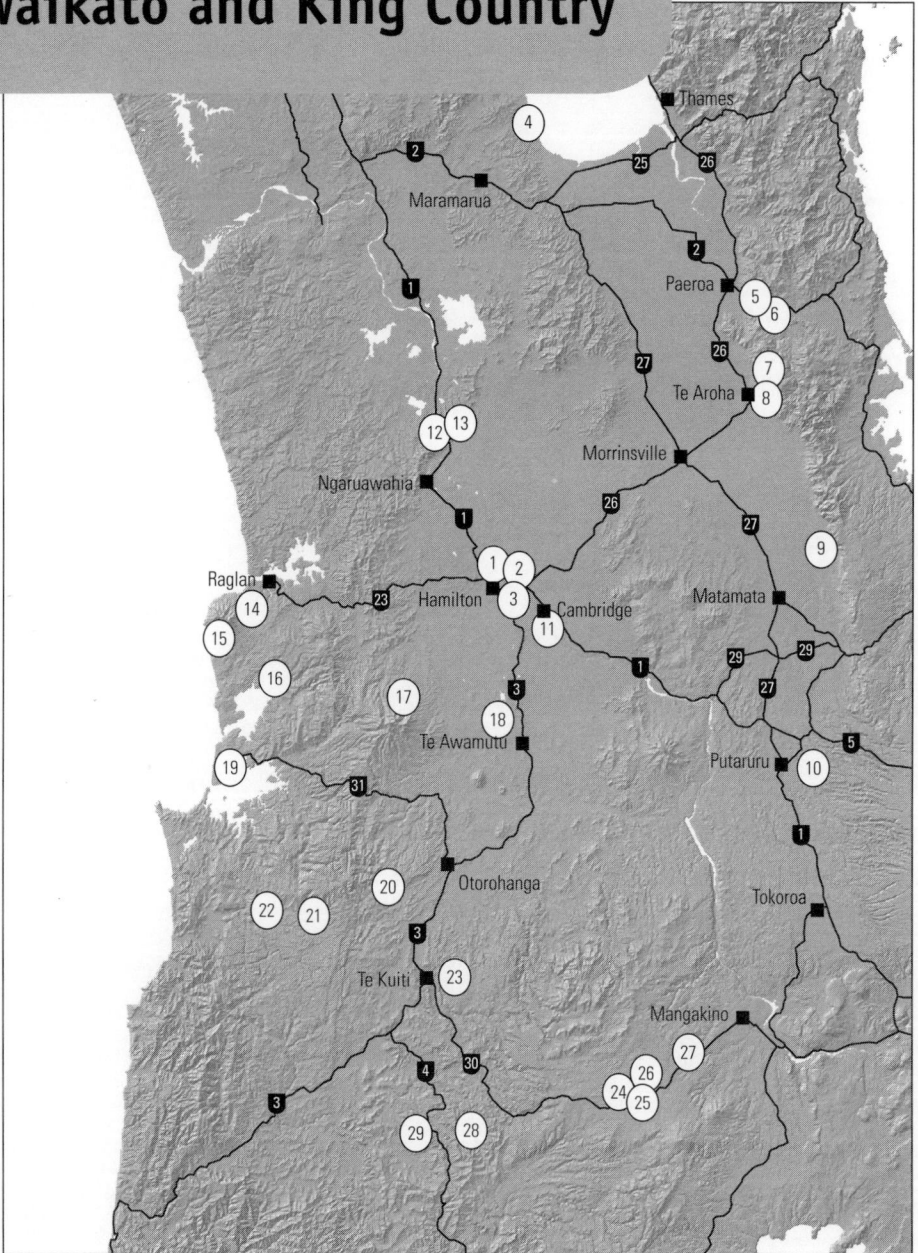

Thames

4

2

Maramarua

25

26

1

2

Paeroa

5
6

27

26

7

Te Aroha

8

12 13

Ngaruawahia

Morrinsville

26

27

1

9

Raglan

1 2

23

Hamilton

3

Cambridge

Matamata

14

11

15

29

29

16

27

17

1

3

18

Te Awamutu

Putaruru

5

19

10

31

1

20

Otorohanga

Tokoroa

22 21

3

Te Kuiti

23

Mangakino

4

30

27

3

26

24 25

29 28

1 Hamilton Gardens   Easy   人   At least 1 hour

- ✳ A stunning and innovative public garden alongside a beautiful stretch of the Waikato River.

- ➤ The gardens are located on SH1 on the eastern side of the river and are well signposted.

Superbly situated on the banks of the Waikato River these 50-hectare gardens are not merely a collection of plants, but focus on plant use, both practical and recreational. The gardens are extensive so if time is short the first stops are the Paradise Gardens representing major historical garden styles: the Japanese Garden of Contemplation, American Modernist Garden, English Flower Garden Border, Italian Renaissance Garden, Indian Char Bagh Garden and Chinese Scholar's Garden. Nearby are the kitchen and herb gardens. The rose gardens are particularly extensive, well laid out in rose types, and are the trial gardens for new breeds prior to general release.

Most of the garden is open all year around; the central theme gardens are open 7.30 am to 6.30 pm in the winter and to 8 pm in the summer. The Victorian Flower Garden Display house is open daily 10 am to 4 pm. The gardens host many special events throughout the year, especially in summer. See their website for details: www.hamiltongardens.co.nz.

2 Jubilee Park   Easy   人   20 minutes

- ✳ A boardwalk leads through a rare remnant of lowland kahikatea forest.

- ➤ Boundary Road, Hamilton.

Known locally as Claudelands Bush, this tiny patch of bush is a poignant reminder of how little remains of the vast lowland forest that once covered the Waikato basin, and which was subsequently cleared and turned into some of the most productive farmland in the world. The boardwalk and fence protect the fragile tree roots and understorey, but unfortunately do not protect the trees from graffiti, the only place in the country where taggers attack native trees in a reserve. The straight-trunked kahikatea are New Zealand's tallest tree, and thrive in damp swampy soils.

3 Waikato River Easy 🚶 1 hour

* ✷ Magnificent old trees line the steep banks of the swiftly flowing Waikato River.

* ➤ While there are numerous access points to the river walks, a good starting
  point is the Waikato Art Museum at the southern end of Victoria Street. There
  is free parking on Grantham Street.

At Hamilton the Waikato River cuts through the surrounding landscape to
create a deep valley through which the waters flow swiftly. In recent years
the city has realised what an asset the river is and has developed an extensive
system of leafy urban walkways along the banks. Complementing and linking
older parks, these walks follow the river under huge old trees that create a
green and pleasant atmosphere in the city the summer months.

From the Waikato Art Museum walk downhill towards the bridge, passing
a small Victorian band rotunda on your right. Above that is the Anglican
Cathedral, occupying the site of the pre-European pa of Kirikiriroa. Take the
steps up to the bridge and cross the river, then return to the river down the
steps to the left. Turn right into Memorial Park, the site of the first landing of
the militia in 1864. Now Hamilton's main war memorial, the park contains
a Spitfire and the anchor of the HMS *Waikato*; it is also home to the paddle
steamer *Waipa Delta*.

Beyond the park follow the street to Jesmond Park and cross the river via
the Claudelands Bridge. Immediately after crossing the river descend back to
the path and follow the river back to the starting point.

4 Miranda Shorebird Centre Easy 🚶 1 hour

* ✷ One of New Zealand's most important and accessible wading and migratory bird
  habitats.

* ➤ The walk begins opposite the Shorebird Centre at 283 East Coast Road,
  Miranda, just south of Kaiaua.

Miranda on the coast of the Firth of Thames is recognised by the Ramsar
Convention as a wetland of international significance. Each year thousands
of birds from the Arctic tundra as well as New Zealand breeding shorebirds
converge on these rich tidal feeding grounds. At high tide the birds are found
on the shell bands and at low tide out feeding on the mudflats.

There are wading birds all year round, but large flocks (7000–10,000) of bar-tailed godwits arrive about September and stay through to March. Known in Russian as *veretennik* ('spindle') on account of their shape, these godwits fly 11,000 km non-stop each year from their nesting grounds in Siberia to New Zealand. Other common birds are the wrybill, New Zealand dotterel, variable oystercatcher, black-billed gull, pied stilt, curlew and sharp-tailed sandpipers, red-necked stint, eastern curlew, banded dotterel and ruddy turnstone.

The walk is over salt marsh, shell banks and tidal mangrove creeks, and hugs the edge of the huge tidal flats. The best time for bird watching is two to three hours either side of high tide, and before heading off it is worth spending a bit of time at the Shorebird Centre which has excellent information on the bird life. For serious birdwatchers there is also a bird hide.

Karangahake Gorge

Once a bustling gold-mining town of more than 5000 people, very little now remains of Karangahake. Across the river three large batteries, the Woodstock, Crown and Talisman, crushed the gold-bearing quartz extracted from mines under Karangahake Mountain. The Victoria Battery at Waikino was the largest in New Zealand, with 200 stampers creating a thumping sound that carried for many miles.

5 Karangahake Gorge: Historic Walkway Loop
Easy 𝕏 1 hour

✳ Railway and gold-mining history combined with a rocky gorge and a wild river.

➤ 8 km east of Paeroa on SH2.

Following the line of the old Paeroa–Waihi Railway, this flat well-formed track runs from Karangahake through to the Waikino Visitor Centre, though the most popular section of the walk is a loop from the car park in the gorge. Beginning over the river, this section of the walk includes the ruins of the Crown Hill, Talisman and Woodstock batteries, a 1-km rail tunnel, the old wooden rail bridge over the Ohinemuri River, and of course the rugged gorge itself. Even though the tunnel is lit, a torch will come in handy as the tunnel lights are at irregular intervals and the track is a bit rough underfoot.

6 Karangahake Gorge: Windows Easy ✝ 30 minutes

✳ Walk the substantial ruins of the Talisman Battery.

➤ 8 km east of Paeroa on SH2.

After crossing the main swing bridge over the Ohinemuri River, cross the second bridge over the Waitawheta River and immediately turn right. This takes you into the substantial ruins of the Talisman Battery. Built in 1901 and closed in 1920, the battery was constructed on a sloping site and this walk covers several levels, with the concrete footings and rusting machinery still in evidence. In 1914 the battery reached its peak, in that one year producing over a quarter-million pounds (in value) of gold. Once you reach the higher level it is worth following the tramline to both left and right. To the left the line finishes at a viewpoint overlooking the Ohinemuri River and the site of the goldmining town of Karangahake, the main street of which was located on the flat where the car park now stands. To the right the line leads to a series of short tunnels, the first of which can be easily negotiated without a torch. A special feature of these tunnels is the 'windows', gaps in the tunnel wall which give dramatic views over a gorge in the Waitawheta River. For the longer tunnel you will need a torch.

7 Mt Te Aroha: Whakapipi or Bald Spur
Hard ✝ 1½ hours return

✳ Great views over Te Aroha and the Hauraki Plains.

➤ The track begins behind the Mokena Geyser in Te Aroha Domain.

A former flourishing spa town, Te Aroha has in recent years successfully renovated its Edwardian domain. Modern hot pools with family appeal complement the historical buildings including the 1898 Cadman Bath House, which now houses the local museum, and the renovated No. 2 Bath House. Restored tearooms and boarding houses complete the picture. At the back of the domain is the Mokena Geyser, the only hot soda-water geyser in the world, which erupts every 40 minutes to a height of around 4 metres. The soda water is reputed to have medicinal qualities.

This track to a lookout point at 350 metres is a good alternative if a trek to the top of the mountain is beyond your reach (952 metres, 2½ hours one

Waikato and
King Country

way). The track zigzags up the hillside through regenerating bush to the great lookout point with excellent views over the town below and the Hauraki Plains beyond. While a steep climb, the track is well formed and not too difficult, and you can reward yourself with a soak in the hot pools afterwards.

8 Howarth Memorial Wetland   Easy 🚶 45 minutes

- ✳ A spooky gothic swamp.
- ➤ Over the old railway bridge at the end of Lawrence Avenue, Te Aroha.

This place is odd. Lying alongside the Waihou River this substantial wetland is mainly planted in exotics, with a few natives added in more recent years. The plantings are eccentric to say the least: a grove of ash trees is laid out in straight lines, there are odd clumps of feijoa, then a line of cherry trees, and large swamp cypress everywhere. Dead trees poke out from the weedy water and the overall effect is of some eerie southern swamp straight out of a gothic horror movie – all that is missing is the 'gators! At least the birds love it, and it is full of ducks, swans and pukeko. But the madness is appealing, and it would make a great place to go for a walk on a moonlit foggy night with strange bird sounds floating out over the black water – if you dare …

9 Wairere Falls   Medium 🚶 1½ hours return to the Falls Lookout

- ✳ One of the highest waterfalls in the North Island.
- ➤ The track to the falls starts at the end of Goodwin Road off the Te Aroha–Okauia Road about 20 km south of Te Aroha.

Set in attractive native bush, these spectacular 153-metre falls drop in two stages over the Okauia Fault. The falls are visible from a wide area of the Waikato, but are hidden for the entire walk only to be finally revealed from the viewing platform. The walk follows the stream, and the bush here is particularly attractive with water trickling down moss- and fern-covered rock faces that in places resemble a Japanese garden. The stream is a testament to the power of water, with huge boulders littering this small valley, some the size of a small car. The walk is a steady uphill grade until you reach a long flight of steps just before the viewing platform. If you want to go to the top of the falls it is a further 45 minutes from this point.

10 Te Waihou Walkway   Easy   🚶   1½ hours one way

⁕ The stunning clear headwaters of the Waihou River flow through a short gorge.

➤ One entrance to the walk is on Whites Road (SH28) between Putaruru and SH5 to Rotorua; the other is 4 km down Leslie Road, which turns off Whites Road to the right just beyond the bridge crossing the Waihou River.

To those familiar with the sluggish dirty brown Waihou River as it flows out to sea by Thames, the headwaters will be nothing short of a shock. The Waihou River begins as the most stunningly pure water, filtered down from the Kaimai Range after being underground for over 50 years. Crystal clear and a brilliant blue-green colour, the stream supports an incredible array of aquatic plants that drift languidly in the transparent water while trout, very easy to spot, swim effortlessly in the swift current. However, think twice before leaping into the water, even on the hottest day, as the water emerges from the Blue Spring at an even 11 degrees all year round.

Most of the walk is through farmland, though there is a small section of bush along the short gorge, and replanting of native trees has occurred in several sections. There is a picnic spot and toilet in the middle of the walk. If you don't have transport at either end or the time or inclination to do the return trip, start the walk at the Leslie Road end as this is the most attractive part of the walk. From this point it will take 40 minutes return to the gorge and 1½ hours return to the two bridges.

11 Te Koutu Lake   Easy   🚶   30 minutes to 1 hour

⁕ An established garden of old trees surrounds a very pretty small lake in the heart of Cambridge.

➤ The main entrance is on Albert Street, Cambridge.

Located in a basin below Cambridge town, Te Koutu Lake is a quiet haven just off SH1 and is an excellent spot to break a journey between Auckland and Rotorua. Established in the 1880s the small lake is surrounded by fine old trees, while on the upper level there are more formal gardens, a conservatory and playgrounds. In summer the water lilies are a particularly attractive sight. A path goes around the lake (this takes about 30 minutes), while a further path circles the park at the upper level.

12 Hakarimata Scenic Reserve   Medium

✳ Massive kauri trees loom over the bush and a lookout gives fantastic views over the lower Waikato.

➤ From SH1 at Huntly cross the Waikato River at the traffic lights and turn left into Riverview Road. Follow the river for 5 km and turn right into Parker Road. The car park is about 500 metres from the turn-off. If arriving from the south, follow the signs from Ngaruawahia.

大 To the kauri: 40 minutes

Lookout: 1½ hours

Near the southern limit of their natural growing area, somehow these magnificent specimens of kauri escaped the logger's axe and stand out boldly from the surrounding bush. The largest tree is estimated to be over 600 years old. While the trees are worth a visit in themselves, it is also worth the uphill grind to the upper lookout. From here there is a magnificent view of the lower Waikato basin, with the river taking centre stage, but also with clear views of Huntly and the surrounding lakes of Waahi, Rotongaro, Hakanoa, Kimihia and Waikare. In the distance far to the north are the Hunua Ranges, Moehau at the top of the Coromandel Peninsula, and on the horizon to the east Mt Te Aroha.

13 Taupiri Mountain Summit   Hard   大 1¼ hours

✳ Fantastic views over the Waikato basin.

➤ The track begins by the small marae just south of Taupiri township where SH1 crosses the Mangawara River. Park by the river and walk to the beginning.

This mountain is tapu (sacred) and should be treated with respect. The track is to the right of the burial grounds, and although it is rough and overgrown the views from the summit are extensive especially to the south. On a crisp sunny winter's day, snow-capped Ruapehu is clearly visible far to the south, while below the Waikato River wends its way through fertile farmland. The track is clearly marked by a wooden arch and is a loop emerging from the bush about 500 metres along the gravel road.

14 Bryant Memorial Scenic Reserve   Easy

✳ Great views over the entrance to Raglan Harbour and far to the north.

➤ From Raglan take the Wainui Road, which eventually changes into Whaanga Road (this is the road to Manu Bay). The reserve is well signposted on the right, though parking can be tricky.

𝅉 Lookout: 20 minutes return

Beach: 40 minutes return

An excellent track leads downhill through attractive bush to a lookout point over Ngarunui Beach, the entrance to Raglan Harbour, and further north along the Waikato coast. This is a good spot to watch surfers trying for waves along Ngarunui Beach. From the viewing platform continue down through the bush to the sand dunes and the long sweep of the beach beyond.

15 Te Toto Gorge Scenic Reserve   Medium 𝅉 30 minutes

✳ Spectacular coastal scenery with Mt Karioi looming above.

➤ From Raglan follow the Wainui and Whaanga Roads around the coast. After Manu Bay the road becomes narrow, winding and unsealed. The car park is on the right 1 km past the sign 'Te Toto Gorge Scenic Reserve'.

Stunted, almost prostrate manuka along this track are testament to the fierce westerly winds that sweep the lower slopes of Mt Karioi, an ancient extinct volcano. The views are superb, both north and south, along the exposed Waikato coastline. The Maori name Te Toto is believed to refer to bloodshed, and there are quiet whispers about the gorge being the scene of a dreadful atrocity in pre-European times.

The track begins at the end of the car park. Although not marked as such, it is reasonably well defined, eventually just petering out in the long grass. How far you want to go is determined by how far uphill you want to walk on the way back.

The track to the Karioi Lookout and Summit (around 3 hours one way) starts on the other side of the road.

16 Bridal Veil Falls Easy

✳ A single fall of over 50 metres drops into a fern-fringed pool.

➤ From SH23, 7 km from Raglan, turn into Te Mata Road. The falls are 13 km down this road, 3 km beyond Te Mata settlement.

🚶 Top of the falls: 15 minutes return
Base of the falls: 25 minutes

One of the Waikato's top scenic attractions, these falls drop 55 metres over a hard layer of basalt into a pool fringed by moisture-loving plants including parataniwha, a native plant with wide nettle-like leaves that in certain seasons turn from green through to shades of light pink and deep red.

The short flat walk from the car park follows the stream. There are two viewing platforms at the top of the falls, though the view from the bottom is more spectacular. The track to the bottom of the falls is being upgraded, but at the time of writing was in places uneven, muddy and slippery. The car park is notorious for car theft so be extra vigilant here, even if there are plenty of cars and people about.

17 Mt Pirongia Medium 🚶 2 hours return to Ruapane Lookout

✳ Fantastic views over the Waikato from a rocky peak high on Pirongia.

➤ The track begins at the car park at the end of Corcoran Road, which is off Te Pahu Road.

Dominating the skyline of the western Waikato is the extinct volcanic cone of Mt Pirongia (959 metres). A legendary stronghold of the wily patupaiarehe (fairy people), this mountain is surprisingly rugged, and the original bush is an unusual mixture of cooler and warmer climate plants. The track to the summit is a slog, but a good alternative is the much easier walk to the Ruapane Lookout at 723 metres. From the car park follow the sign that says 'Picnic Area and Lookout'; the Ruapane track peels off to the left about 30 metres into the bush. The track is a gradual climb, some of it through fine tawa forest, but not far from Ruapane the track becomes steeper before arriving at a well-defined rocky outcrop giving a fantastic view back over the lush Waikato. Beyond Ruapane the track leads to another rocky outcrop called Tirohanga with even better views (about 30 minutes further).

18 Yarndley's Bush Easy 🚶 30 minutes

✳ The largest remnant of kahikatea forest in the Waikato.

➤ 4 km north of Te Awamutu turn left off SH4 into Ngaroto Road. The reserve is 1 km on the left.

At 14 hectares this is the largest remaining lowland bush in the Waikato and, unusually, it consists almost totally of kahikatea. On entering the reserve the immediate impression is not of native bush but of a pine forest, and it is easy to see why kahikatea was called white pine by early Europeans. The trunks are straight and clean, topped by conifer-like foliage with only the buttress-shaped roots being a telltale sign that these are trees of the wetland. A drop in the water table through drainage of nearby farmland has left the distinctive kahikatea root system more exposed than normal.

The walkway has extensive boardwalks to protect the fragile roots, and a viewing platform allows at least a partial bird's-eye view of the forest.

19 Te Puia Hot Springs Easy 🚶 20 minutes return

✳ A hot-water spring in the middle of a windswept beach.

➤ From Kawhia township take Te Puia Road out to the beach. The short walk to the beach is through the pine trees by the car park.

Not a beach for improving your tan, but ideal for surfcasting and taking a long walk along empty wild sands to blow away any cares or worries. Accessible for 2 hours either side of low tide are hot water springs, which are situated directly out from the main track to the beach from the car park. This beach is exposed to the westerly wind, so bring a substantial digging tool to make a protective wall around your very own hot pool in the sand.

20 Ruakuri Walkway   Easy 𐀪 30 minutes

✳ Limestone caves, arches and caverns interwoven with native bush.

➤ 2 km from the Waitomo Glow-worm Caves, next to the entry to Aranui Cave.

The short walk along the Waitomo River is crammed with fantastic limestone outcrops, caves and a huge natural tunnel. The unspoiled bush features luxuriant growth, in particular ferns, mosses and lichens. Easy to miss is the wonderful underground cavern which is about 5 metres past the natural bridge viewing platform. Initially it appears to be no more than a hole in the ground, but let your eyes adjust and the short flight of steps quickly becomes apparent. These lead to a lookout point in a huge cavern high above the river as it disappears underground.

The area has glow-worms at night, but don't forget your torch. The track is well formed, but walk the track anticlockwise or else the signs won't quite make sense.

21 Mangapohue Natural Bridge   Easy

✳ Two natural bridges in a bush-lined gorge.

➤ 26 km from Waitomo on Te Anga Road.

𐀪 Natural bridges: 20 minutes return
Bridges via the fossils: 30 minutes return

Just a short distance from the road are two magnificent natural limestone arches, one on top of the other, created by the waters of the Mangapohue Stream. The walk to the arches is through an attractive gorge lined with ferns and mosses; at night there are glow-worms (a torch is necessary if a night walk is planned). Beyond the bridges the track continues out into open farmland, and returns to the road via large rocky outcrops containing the fossilised remains of gigantic oysters from a time when this land was submerged under the sea.

22 Marokopa Falls Easy 🚶 20 minutes return

* ✳ A magnificent waterfall hidden in luxuriant bush.

* ✳ 31 km from Waitomo on Te Anga Road.

A short walk through cool lush bush leads to the falls where the Marokopa River cascades 30 metres, creating a spectacular waterfall. Only a short walk from the road, these falls, together with the Mangapohue natural bridge on the same road, are worth the detour from a visit to the Waitomo Caves.

23 Mangaokewa Gorge Scenic Reserve Easy

* ✳ A clear stream runs through bush along a limestone gorge.

* ➤ 2 km south of Te Kuiti on SH30 (road to Mangakino).

* 🚶 Cascade: 40 minutes return
  Waterfall: 1¼ hours return

Set in a deep gorge just south of Te Kuiti, this reserve features huge limestone bluffs towering above a stream flanked by mature native bush containing large tawa, rimu and kahikatea. For a pleasant change native birdlife, particularly kereru (New Zealand pigeon), is common. Begin by crossing the swing bridge by the car park and following the stream, first to an attractive cascade, and further on to a small waterfall. You need to return the same way as there is only a very rough track on the other side. An added bonus is the many swimming holes, just the thing on a hot summer's day.

Pureora Forest

This superb forest has an interesting history. The whole thing was flattened in the Taupo eruption 1800 years ago; more recently it came under threat from loggers, but was saved from the axe in 1978 by protesters who perched themselves on platforms in the trees. Logging finally halted in the 1980s and the area is currently a combination of forest park and commercial forest, which makes for some interesting contrasts between pristine native bush and clear-felled pine forest.

Today there are numerous short walks in the park, though some of them are accessible only from the fringes. It is also worth noting that the roads in the forest are narrow metalled forestry roads, some little better than tracks and very rough in parts. The following three walks begin at or near the Pureora Visitor Centre, which is 3 km down Barryville Road (SH30), 56 km from Te Kuiti and 20 km from Mangakino.

24 Pureora Forest: Totara Walk Easy ⅄ 25 minutes

* ✱ Huge native trees hundreds of years old and absolutely magnificent.

* ➤ The beginning of the walk is 200 metres from the Pureora Visitor Centre.

Walking through this forest it is easy to see what motivated both conservationists and loggers. A mixture of totara, maire, rimu and tawa, it contains some truly huge trees, the height and size of which must be seen to be believed.

25 Pureora Forest: Buried Forest Easy ⅄ 5 minutes

* ✱ A couple of old logs.

* ➤ If you really want to go, the turn-off to the Buried Forest is 2 km from the Pureora Visitor Centre on Barryville Road.

The idea of a buried forest is much more exciting than the reality, and in fact this must be one of the dullest sights in New Zealand. First you must travel along a rutted narrow gravel forestry road to take a short walk through blackberry-infested pine forest to view a couple of half-buried old logs with absolutely no redeeming features. Rather than being labelled the 'buried forest' it should really be called 'a half-buried old log or two'.

What *is* fascinating is the event that caused the forest to be flattened. Over 1800 years ago a cataclysmic eruption blew out the western side of Lake Taupo, over 70 km away. Even at this distance the force of the blast was so strong that it destroyed the entire forest in the area, knocking over huge mature trees and then burying them under a deep layer of ash and pumice. Part of this forest was accidentally uncovered in the 1970s, and a couple of ancient preserved logs can be seen along this short track.

26 Pureora Forest: Forest Tower Track

Easy 🚶 10 minutes return

✹ A wooden tower allows a unique view of the forest canopy.

➤ 2 km from the Pureora Visitor Centre on Barryville Road.

A short flat track leads to a 12-metre tower which gives an excellent view over the forest treetops and, with a bit of patience, some of the birdlife in the area. This area is where the conservationists made their stand by securing themselves high in the trees selected to be felled (see page 76). At the time the policy was one of selective logging, in which a proportion of mature trees were felled and then removed along the access road which is now the track. The area between the car park and the tower has been subjected to selective logging, while the area on the other side of the tower is still pristine. The difference is plain to see. It is easy in a more conservation-minded age to label the loggers as greedy and insensitive to the environment, but in many areas milling was the only source of work, and cessation of felling meant a loss of valuable jobs in an area where no other employment was available.

27 Poukani – the world's largest totara

Easy 🚶 40 minutes return

✹ A totara tree over 40 metres tall.

➤ The entrance to the track is 10 km from the Barryville Road turn-off towards Mangakino, and 12 km from Mangakino on SH30.

While thousands of visitors flock to Tane Mahuta (see page 27), this tree is hardly known and rarely visited – and yet it is so impressive. Poukani is a giant tree over 42 metres tall and estimated to be 1800 years old. Its rivals, the second and third largest totara trees, are both located in nearby Pureora Forest. The walk to the tree is through a handsome forest of wheki (tree fern) with a sprinkling of larger trees, and although the track is not marked it is reasonably well defined.

28 Mapara Scenic Reserve Medium 🚶 1 hour return

✳ The most accessible and important stronghold of the kokako.

➤ Travel 26 km south of Te Kuiti on SH4 and turn left into Kopaki Road. After 2 km turn right into Mapara South Road. The reserve is 5.5 km down this gravel road.

One of the last strongholds of the rare kokako, this reserve is the most accessible for those who want to hear or see this elusive and attractive bird whose song is so distinct. With persistent trapping of predators the kokako numbers in the reserve had rocketed to 77 breeding pairs in 2006.

The track in the reserve leads through the territories of several birds, so the chance of hearing them is very high, but you will need to be patient to actually see a bird. The best chance is the period two hours after dawn; you just have to get up very early, especially in summer.

29 Omaru Falls Easy 🚶 1 hour return

✳ A pleasant bush walk leads to a splendid, but little-visited waterfall.

➤ 30 km south of Te Kuiti on SH4 turn into Omaru Road. The falls are 500 metres down this road. There is a small sign and it is easy to miss.

Despite their handy location just off the main highway south of Te Kuiti and a flat walk all the way, these falls are not well known. The Mapiu Stream plunges 50 metres over a hard basalt lip into a rocky pool and after heavy rain the falls are spectacular. The walk follows the stream through farmland and regenerating bush with some huge kahikatea, and eventually crosses the stream over a rickety swing bridge. The viewing platform is high above the falls, which gives the visitor an excellent view, though there is no access to the pool below the falls.

Waikato and King Country

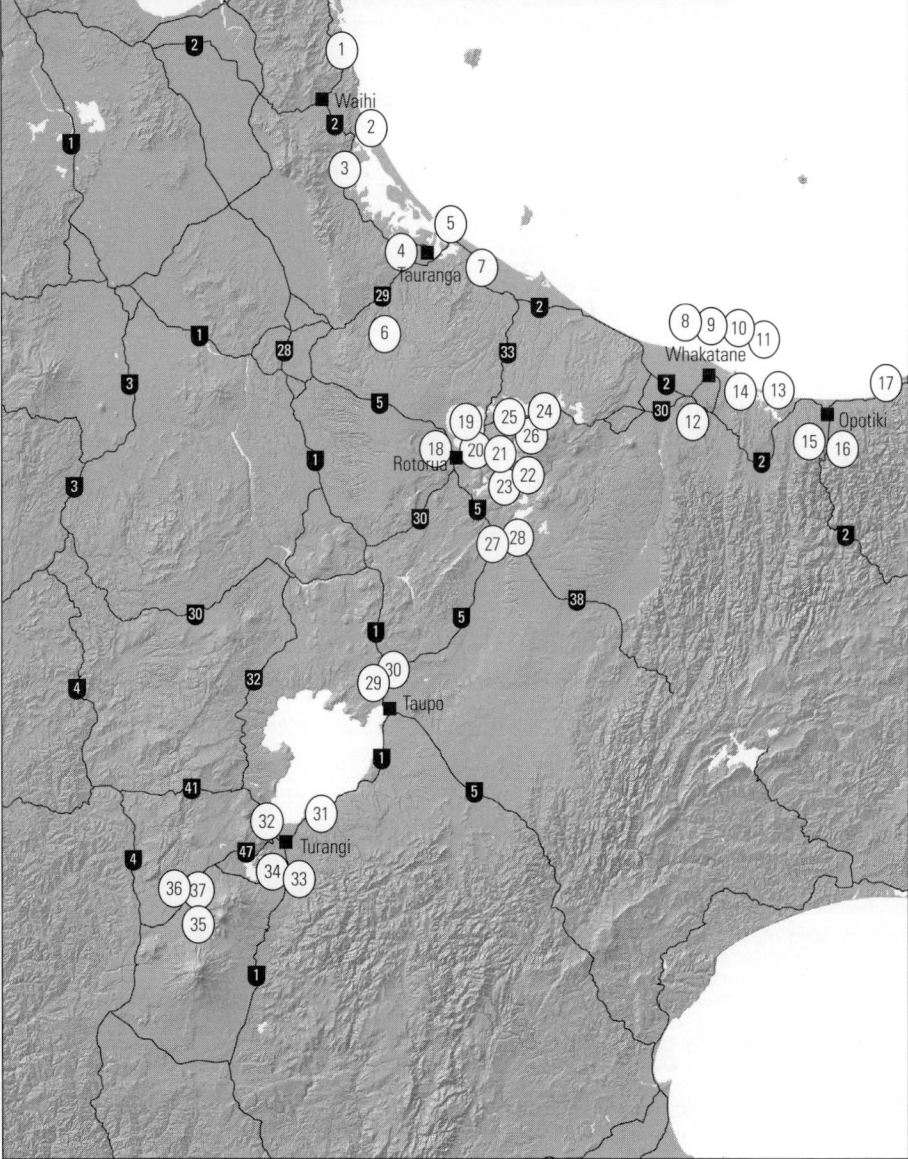

1 Orokawa Bay   Medium   𐀀   1½ hours return

* A beautiful sandy beach backed by old pohutukawa trees.

➤ The track begins at the northern end of Waihi Beach by the Surf Club. At very high tide it can be tricky to access the track.

Climbing along the coast from Waihi Beach, this excellent track winds its way through regenerating bush to a magical bay that is as close to perfect as you can get. Crystal-clear water rushes on to a wide sweep of sand that is fringed with ancient pohutukawa trees, ideal shade on a hot summer's day. A short distance from the beach are the 28-metre-high William Wright Falls (30 minutes return). For the fit a track leads north to another sandy beach, Homunga Bay, though this is another 2 hours return from Orokawa, and the track is not so well formed.

The surf can be rough here at times so take care when swimming, and there are occasional stingrays in the shallow waters.

2 Bowentown Heads   Easy   𐀀   1 hour

* Old pa sites crown these small hills at the entrance to Tauranga Harbour.

➤ From Waihi Beach township follow the road along the beach south to the heads.

From a distance Bowentown Heads look like one entity, but they are in fact distinct hills. Both topped by ancient pa sites, the hills protect the Katikati entrance to Tauranga Harbour, and have excellent views north along Waihi Beach, and south over Matakana Island to Mt Maunganui. Offshore Mayor Island is clearly visible, while the view to the west is of fertile farmland backed by the bush-clad Kaimai Range.

From the upper car park it is a 20-minute return steep climb to the top, and just to the west of the car park the defensive ditches of the old pa site are plain to see. A short steep path drops down to Cave Bay, a beautiful small sandy beach overhung with pohutukawa, though take care when swimming as the tidal flow through the entrance can be fierce. On the inland side of the heads, Anzac Bay is safer for swimming and from this point the second, smaller hill, also with a pa site, is more easily accessible.

3 Haiku Walk Easy 人 As long as you need

＊ A gentle stroll in a river park contemplating haiku.

➤ On SH2 in Katikati, the entrance is next to the Mitre 10 in the main shopping centre.

Rather than just establish yet another walk by a river, the residents of Katikati have been particularly clever. As well as providing a pleasant open space they have added haiku on rocks and stones in the riverside park behind the shops in the centre of town. Haiku are 17-syllable poems consisting of three lines of five, seven and five syllables. The world's shortest form of poetry, haiku was established as a great literary form in Japan and is used to express profound truths in the simplest images. It is ideally suited to the natural environment and finds a perfect home in this park.

4 Te Puna Quarry Park Easy 人 1 hour

＊ Huge fun in this clever mix of formal garden, art and old machinery in an abandoned quarry.

➤ Quarry Road, off SH2 at Te Puna, north of Tauranga.

At Te Puna, just north of Tauranga, local residents banded together to form Te Puna Quarry Park, and have created a whimsical and delightful garden in an old abandoned quarry. Leaving some of the quarry infrastructure and machinery intact, the Society has added gardens and art work that even the meanest and hardest heart will enjoy. In the car park is an old storybook-like digger that children can play on, while the gardens include heritage roses, vireya rhododendrons, bromeliads, succulents, South African plants and even a small kauri grove.

The more formal plantings are on the lower area near the car park, while from the higher terraces there are excellent views over the Bay of Plenty and a small contemplative oriental garden.

Over 30 pieces of art work are spread around the gardens including stylised sculptures of Hinuera stone, pottery and a fabulous mosaic family grouping, complete with a small dog. Children in the know head straight for the outdoor percussion area, where young and old can bang and crash to their hearts' content on a variety of 'instruments'.

The gardens are fairly new so are a bit rough in parts, but the quarry setting means absolutely no mud and happy dry feet.

5 Mt Maunganui/Mauao

✻ Spectacular views of the Bay of Plenty from this extinct volcano.

➤ The track begins in Mt Maunganui on the corner of Adams Terrace and Marine Parade.

Mt Maunganui/Mauao is an extinct volcano with much of its outer material long since eroded to leave the harder lava core exposed, forming dramatic rampart-like rock formations just below the summit.

That's the official version, but the Maori legend of the origin of the mountain is much more endearing. Mauao, originally a nameless slave, formerly lived in the foothills of the Kaimai Range, and was desperately in love with beautiful Puwhenua. However, Puwhenua did not return his love and instead was in love with the handsome Otanewainuku. Unable to endure the torment of seeing his beloved with another, the nameless one decided to kill himself by flinging himself into the ocean and drowning. The lovesick mountain was dragged to the sea by the patupaiarehe (fairy people), whom he called on to help him. It was a long slow haul through the night, and soon it was dawn. The patupaiarehe, fearful of being caught by the sun's rays, fled back to their forest, leaving the hapless mountain who became Mauao, 'caught by the morning sun'. Now forever trapped on the edge of the sea, Mauao gazes back at his lost love Puwhenua in the arms of his rival.

Base track   Easy ⅄ 45 minutes

The base track follows the coastline around on a broad undulating path that is popular with walkers and runners, old and young alike. From the superb surf of the main beach the track skirts the rocky shoreline pounded by the open sea, and winds around to the entrance of the harbour, busy with both pleasure craft and commercial fishing boats. If you are in luck you will see a container or logging ship working its way through the harbour entrance. Overhung with old pohutukawa, the track continues around to the sheltered waters of Pilot Bay, passing the statue of Tangaroa, god of the sea, and an historic stone jetty.

Summit track   Medium 🚶 1¼ hours return

The information boards at the beginning of the walks show a confusing number of tracks to and around the summit. In reality it is much simpler than it looks, and while it is a steady climb to the 232-metre peak the tracks are mostly in excellent condition and not that difficult. After passing through the camping ground and the gate, the track immediately leads off uphill to the left. At the junction there are two options for reaching the summit, with the Oruahine track a more gentle grade than the steeper Waikorere track. On the summit the views are dramatic, along the coast with views out to Mayor Island, inland to the Kaimai Range, and with Tauranga, Mt Maunganui town and Matakana Island spread below. The summit is a surprising area of flattish land, and the remains of an old pa are visible around the trig point. The return down the mountain is via the 4WD track, which goes down the harbour side of the mountain and exits at the Pilot Bay end of Adams Avenue.

6 Omanawa Falls   Easy 🚶 30 minutes return

✳ A stunning waterfall drops into an equally stunning pool.

➤ On the Lower Kaimai Road into Tauranga (SH29) turn into Omanawa Road and drive 11 km to the car park.

The Omanawa Falls plunge dramatically over a bluff in a single drop into a broad pool of dark blue-green water. It is a pity these falls are not more accessible as they are particularly attractive. Poorly signposted, the track goes down through a bushy glade to a barely adequate lookout point, and the track can be slippery if it is wet. The mysterious green door at the end of the path doesn't lead to an alternative world or anywhere that exciting – it was the access to an old power station established in 1915.

7 Papamoa Hills Regional Park Summit

Medium 🚶 1 hour 15 minutes

- ✳ Spectacular views over the Bay of Plenty and the impressive remains of an old pa site.

- ➤ Some 5 km north of Te Puke on SH2 turn left into Poplar Lane and drive 800 metres to the car park.

A steady uphill track, this walk begins through a mature pine forest with an unusual understorey made up almost entirely of kawakawa. Take some time to chew a small piece of a new leaf and enjoy the peppery taste followed by a mild numbness as you experience the anaesthetising effect of this plant. Early herbalists used this plant to alleviate toothache by packing the infected tooth with kawakawa leaf and thereby numbing the pain.

The trail eventually emerges from the trees to open farmland with increasingly broad views of the eastern Bay of Plenty. The spectacular views to the west are only revealed just before the trig point on the summit (224 metres). This is the site of Karangaumu, an impressive pa and one of seven in the park. Not only is it a large pa, covering the entire summit, but the ramparts, defensive ditches and terraces are all clearly visible. Even to eyes untrained in military matters the strategic advantage of this hilltop pa is immediately obvious. The whole bay is clearly visible and watchful lookouts would have missed nothing from this ancient fortress. The track is particularly well maintained and well signposted.

Nga Tapuwae O Toi

This popular walkway is 17 km long and takes 7 hours to complete, well outside the scope of this book. The most popular section is from Whakatane to Ohope, which takes around 2½ hours one way, though part of the track is tide dependent. If you don't have return transport there is a bus service from Ohope back to Whakatane, but before you start check with the Information Centre on both the tides and the bus timetables.

The following three walks are short sections of the walkway that can be completed in a much shorter space of time.

Bay of Plenty, Rotorua, Taupo and central North Island

8 Nga Tapuwae O Toi: Ohope to Otarawairere Beach
Medium

✳ A beautiful sandy beach fringed by old pohutukawa.

➤ At the bottom of the hill on the road from Whakatane just as it enters Ohope, turn left into West End Road and go to the end. Walk along the beach towards the headland; the track starts at the base of the hill.

🚶 Lookout: 25 minutes return

Beach: 1 hour return

The track begins steadily uphill (there are some steps), with Ohope and the eastern Bay of Plenty stretching out in the distance framed by native bush including old pohutukawa. The views are even better from the lookout, where the track then drops steeply down to Otarawairere Bay. This sheltered sand and shell beach is enclosed by rocky headlands and overhung by huge pohutukawa trees, making it the ideal destination on a warm summer's day or for an early morning walk.

9 Nga Tapuwae O Toi: Kapu Te Rangi/Toi's Pa
Medium 🚶 45 minutes return from Seaview Road

✳ Excellent views of the eastern Bay of Plenty from this ancient pa.

➤ The walk begins from the car park on Seaview Road in Whakatane; if walking up from the town, take the long flight of steps in Canning Place behind Pohaturoa Rock.

Toi was one of Polynesia's greatest voyagers, not only exploring the coastline of New Zealand, but repeatedly crossing back and forward across the South Pacific. Kapu Te Rangi is one of New Zealand's oldest pa sites and the strategic value of this hilltop location is obvious. The views are endless in all directions, and with the steep drop on the river side of the pa, the site was eminently defendable. It was Toi's pa that the male crew members of the Mataatua waka were visiting when it slipped its moorings and was saved by the actions of Wairaka (see the Historic Whakatane River walk on the next page).

The track is in excellent condition with some stepped sections. At the very beginning the walk crosses the top of Wairere Falls.

10 Nga Tapuwae O Toi: Fairbrother Loop Walk

Medium 🚶 1¼ hours

* Stroll through an impressive pohutukawa forest.

➤ The walk is on the right just as you enter Ohope from Whakatane. The start of the track is marked by an arch.

While the traditional picture of pohutukawa is a gnarled old tree overhanging a beach or high on a cliff face, it is also in fact a tree of the forest. Here its growth habit is much more upright, less spreading, drawn up by the other trees of the forest to reach some surprising heights. This loop walk is through such a forest, dense with tall pohutukawa from saplings through to ancient trees. There is no lookout point along this track, though the sea is occasionally glimpsed through the trees.

11 Historic Whakatane River Easy 🚶 1 hour

* Maori and Pakeha history are intertwined on this attractive walk along the Whakatane River.

➤ Start the walk at the Information Centre on Kakahoroa Drive, Whakatane.

Toroa, the captain of the famous waka Mataatua, was given instructions by his father Irakewa before leaving Hawaiki to look for three distinct landmarks that would mark the place to settle. These landmarks are still visible 800 years later within the central business area of Whakatane and linked by a walk. The first landmark is Muriwai's Cave (partially collapsed), where Irakewa's daughter lived, and was highly tapu until 1963 when the tapu was lifted. The second is Wairere Falls; while not so spectacular this is nonetheless attractive for a waterfall right in the middle of town. And finally, Pohaturoa Rock contains a highly tapu cave where tohunga performed sacred ceremonies.

When the waka Mataatua, captained by Toroa, arrived and moored in the estuary, the men climbed up to Kapu Te Rangi, leaving the women and children behind on the Mataatua. A swift outgoing tide put the waka in danger of being carried out to sea but, in a breach of tradition, Toroa's daughter Wairaka saved the day by picking up a paddle and exclaiming 'E! Kia whakatane au i ahau' ('Let me act like a man'), and with the other women brought the waka back to safety. This action is the origin of the name of both the river and the town.

Start the walk by the Information Centre and follow the river towards the sea past the busy Whakatane Wharf, home to both commercial and pleasure boats, and on to the landing place of the Mataatua and a replica of this famous waka. From here continue to the heads and the bronze statue of Wairaka overlooking the narrow entrance to the river. Follow the road back to town, taking in Toroa's three landmarks – Muriwai's Cave, Wairere Falls and Pohaturoa Rock – in the very centre of the business area.

12 White Pine Bush   Easy   人   20 minutes

✳ Impressive mature kahikatea in this rare forest remnant.

➤ White Pine Bush Road (SH2), 20 km south of Whakatane.

A tiny 4.5-hectare reserve is all that remains of the dense lowland forest that once covered this plain. Huge kahikatea dominate and it is from these trees that the reserve takes its name. Kahikatea were known to early European settlers as white pine, though they do not belong to the pine family, because forests of pure kahikatea have the distinct feel of a pine forest. Kahikatea is a very pale timber and was extensively used to make butter boxes as the wood was both light and readily available, and did not taint the butter.

13 Ohiwa Harbour: Sandspit Wildlife Refuge
Easy   人   1½ hours

✳ An important tidal sanctuary for migratory wading birds.

➤ Follow Harbour Road right to the very end just beyond the boat ramp where there is a sign indicating the refuge.

Ohiwa Harbour is very tidal. With over 70 per cent of the harbour seabed exposed at low tide, it is one of the most important refuges for migratory wading birds including, among others, the bar-tailed godwit (which flies non-stop from the Arctic each spring), the New Zealand dotterel, banded dotterel and variable oystercatcher. While there are reserves on both entrances to the harbour, this one is on the western (Ohope) side.

Unfortunately there is no helpful signage or map at the beginning of the area and the only track is a 4WD access road through the middle of the dunes, which is not at all helpful if you are here to see the birds. The following walk is mainly coastal, which will prevent you from getting too lost.

From the car park follow the grass track along the coast to a point about 500 metres past the golf course where the track splits. Take the right-hand track down onto the sand, then follow the sand all the way round to the harbour entrance and the open sea beach. This area is the main birdwatching site, with wading birds favouring the tidal flats and nesting seabirds occupying the sand above high tide. On the ocean side, continue around until you see an old fence post on the dunes to your left. Just to the right of this fence post is the 4WD track that leads back to the car park.

14 Tuwhare Pa Easy 人 15 minutes return

* Historically important pa site with great views.

➤ The track is on the right 200 metres from the Ohope Beach/Opotiki Road intersection.

Ohiwa Harbour was the traditional boundary between two tribes, Ngati Awa to the west and Whakatohea to the east. While Whakatohea claimed the entire harbour, this important Ngati Awa pa reinforced their claim to important and rich food resources. Tuwhare pa is in fact three distinct pa sites, all in very close proximity, and with views over the harbour and the sea the strategic position is obvious.

15 Hukutaia Domain/Burial Tree Easy 人 30 minutes

* A 2000-year-old puriri tree formerly used to hold the bones of the dead.

➤ From Opotiki take the road to Whakatane. Just over the Waioeka River bridge turn left into Woodlands Road. The reserve is on the left 7 km down this road.

This small reserve of low rainforest was established in 1918 primarily to protect Taketakerau, an ancient puriri tree. The tree was used by the local Upokorehe hapu to conceal the bones of the notable dead from desecration by enemies, though after the tree was damaged the remains were buried elsewhere. Thought to be over 2000 years old, this huge tree is highly tapu.

From 1933 to 1970 local amateur botanist Norman Potts travelled throughout New Zealand to gather plants for the Hukutaia Domain, and thereby created one of the most extensive collections of native trees and shrubs in the country. His work was continued by Marc Heginbotham from 1970 to 1990.

The tracks are not well marked, but the reserve is very small and you can't get lost, though the puriri tree might take a little searching out.

16 Marawaiwai   Easy   𝘟   5 minutes

* A fine remnant of virgin lowland forest.

➤ From Opotiki take SH2 towards Gisborne. After 5 km turn left into Warrington Road, then right into Harrison Road. The reserve is on the right 2 km down Harrison Road.

Huge kahikatea dominate this rare reserve of lowland forest, which is easily accessible on this flat loop walk. There is good interpretive signage to help identify native plants. A very pleasant grassy picnic spot at the entrance to the reserve adds to the appeal.

17 Tauturangi Walkway   Easy   𝘟   50 minutes return

* Fine views over the Bay of Plenty and the East Cape.

➤ 10 km east of Opotiki on SH35 turn left into Opape Beach Road. Park down by the beach.

This well-formed track leads up and around a coastal headland with excellent views out to Whale and White Islands and further along the rugged bush-clad East Cape coast. The walkway also passes the old pa sites of Kohinehine, Ruruarama and Tarakeha.

To access the track go down the boat ramp and walk along the beach. The beginning of the walk is just over the stream. The track stops just beyond the lookout so there is not much point going any further. Park on the road to the left of the boat ramp so the ramp is left clear for those launching boats.

18 Rotorua City Easy 🚶 1 hour

✳ Rotorua's key historic buildings and thermal surprises.

➤ Government Gardens, Fenton Street, Rotorua.

Begin the walk from the Government Gardens in Fenton Street. These superb gardens were established on land gifted by Ngati Whakaue 'for the benefit of the people of the world'. Developed at the end of the 19th century, the park contains formal gardens, historic sites and hot water springs, and is linked through to the lake-front park. Highlights are the striking Government Bath House, the Blue Baths and the Polynesian Spa. Note that the thermal areas on the lake edge are unpredictable and visitors should always stay on the marked paths. The distinctive arch marking the entrance at the eastern end of Arawa Street was built of totara to celebrate the visit of the Duke and Duchess of Cornwall in 1901, and originally stood at the intersection of Hinemoa and Fenton Streets.

The lawn bowls and croquet green in front of the Government Bath House creates a uniquely genteel picture and is complemented by the beautifully restored 1903 Edwardian tea pavilion overlooking it.

From the Government Gardens walk through to the lake front, which is the starting point for trips out onto the lake, including Mokoia Island, and the base for float-plane excursions. Noted for its over-friendly black swans, the park here is also the location for the popular *Opera in the Pa* concerts.

Continue west along the lake front to Ohinemutu Village. One of the most important Ngati Whakaue settlements, Ohinemutu has been the heart of Maori Rotorua for hundreds of years. Overlooking the lake is St Faith's Church, built in 1910 with Tudor-style overtones, and the interior is decorated with fine weaving and paintings. Of special note is the window showing Christ as a Maori chief, placed in such a way that he appears to be walking on the waters of Lake Rotorua. Services on Sunday are held in English and Maori. Behind the church are the graves of returned soldiers buried above ground as the area is too hot for burials underground.

Ohinemutu also houses the beautifully carved meeting house Tama Te Kapua on the Te Papa-I-Ouru marae, named after the captain of the waka Arawa, Tama Te Kapua, who brought the ancestors of the Arawa iwi to Aotearoa around AD 1350. Ohinemutu is a contemporary Maori community, not a tourist attraction, and while the local people welcome visitors every

Bay of Plenty,
Rotorua, Taupo and
central North Island

respect should be shown to both people and places.

From St Faith's continue west past fine carved meeting houses and veer left into Ariariterangi Street, where steam floats up from stormwater drains, and hot water bubbles in backyards. Then turn left into Rangipahere Street, which leads to Kuirau Park. Thermal activity is concentrated in the north-eastern section of the park, but this is an area of increasing thermal activity and may vary considerably from year to year and season to season. In the more formal area of the park by the children's play area there are two small shallow pools especially designed for soaking tired feet. From here cross the road to Arawa Street, which leads back to the Government Gardens.

19 Mokoia Island   Medium 人 2 hours

* An historic island and also a significant bird sanctuary.

➤ Only guided tours go to the island. Contact Mokoia Island Wai Ora Experiences, Memorial Drive, Lakefront, Rotorua (www.mokoiaisland.co.nz, phone 07 349 0976).

Occupied by the Te Arawa iwi for over 700 years, Mokoia Island was prized as a strategic defensive site and a rich fertile area for growing the valuable kumara. Of particular fame is the great love story of Hinemoa and Tutanekai. Hinemoa, forbidden by her family to marry the handsome warrior Tutanekai, swam at night from the shores of the lake to the island guided only by the sound of Tutanekai's flute (now in the Rotorua museum). On reaching the island Hinemoa warmed herself in a hot pool, now known (not surprisingly) as Hinemoa's Pool. In later years the island was considered too isolated and the last residents left in 1953.

Now a bird sanctuary, Mokoia Island is an excellent place to see rare birds such as the saddleback, hihi (stitchbird), brown teal and North Island weka. In addition to the conservation area, historic areas include the site of Tutanekai's whare, Hinemoa's Pool (which the visitor can swim in) and an ancient stone carving of the kumara god.

Easy tracks cover the island and a guided walk option is available.

20 The Redwoods/Whakarewarewa Forest

Easy   🚶   30 minutes to 1¼ hours or more, depending on the track

* ✳ Magnificent groves of redwoods and other exotic trees.

* ➤ Take Te Ngae Road from Rotorua towards Te Puke and Whakatane, and turn right into Tarawera Road. The turn-off to the redwoods is immediately to the right and the beginning of the walk is on the left 500 metres down this road.

This forest is hugely popular with runners, mountain bikers and walkers, and its highlight is the extensive grove of mighty redwood trees planted as part of early forestry experiments, though there are also extensive areas of Douglas fir, larch and even a grove of plane trees. Officially known as the Whakarewarewa Forest, but popularly referred to as just The Redwoods, the forest stretches from Rotorua city right through to the Blue and Green Lakes, and is a complex maze of tracks that can take from 30 minutes to all day.

Three short loop tracks start from behind and to the right of the Visitor Centre, all very well formed, though the longest loop has a bit more uphill. If you want to avoid the coach loads that pack these walks during the day, try to visit either earlier in the morning or later in the afternoon. This is a lovely place to visit on a quiet summer's evening when you can picnic on the grass in the old quarry. There are separate tracks for mountain bikes.

21 Okareka Walkway   Easy

* ✳ An excellent lakeside wetland walk.

* ➤ From SH30 turn into Te Ngae Road and then into Tarawera Road. Turn left into Lake Okareka Loop Road, and at the lake turn left into Acacia Road. The walk is signposted to the left.

* 🚶 End of the boardwalk: 30 minutes return
  Okareka outlet: 1½ hours

This newly opened track leads downhill to a broad wetland valley on the fringes of Lake Okareka, and the open nature of the landscape makes it quite different to the other Rotorua lakes. A wide boardwalk crosses a marshland of sedges, rushes and raupo to a specially constructed hide for the more serious birdwatchers. Black swans, pukeko, shags, ducks and stilts are among the many birds that feed in the shallow wetland.

22 Lake Tarawera   Easy   🚶   15 minutes return

✳ Mt Tarawera lies across the lake from two sandy beaches and Maori rock art.

➤ From SH30 turn into Te Ngae Road and then into Tarawera Road, and follow the road all the way to Tarawera Landing, 2 km past the Buried Village.

This large lake of beautiful clear water, renowned for its trout fishing, lies at the foot of Mt Tarawera and was substantially altered by the 1886 eruption. Nine days prior to the eruption a mysterious waka was seen on the lake by a party of tourists returning from the Terraces, but as their waka approached the boat it suddenly disappeared. It was believed by many to be a waka wairua (spirit canoe) warning of the approaching doom, and it is said that a reappearance of the waka will signal the next eruption.

The access point to the walk at Tarawera Landing has a small sandy beach, a boat ramp and a café. To the right of the car park is a short walk to the Wairoa Stream, the outlet for the Green Lake, and to the left another short walk leads to Maori rock drawings. These drawings were originally covered by the 1886 eruption but rediscovered in 1904. Executed in korowai or red ochre, the drawings are indistinct but depict a waka motif. Continue past the drawings and through the large grassed area to a small sandy beach; if the main beach is crowded you can always find a tranquil spot here.

23 Blue and Green Lakes   Easy   🚶   1½ hours

✳ A lakeside walk around the Blue Lake with views over the Green Lake.

➤ From SH30 turn into Te Ngae Road and then into Tarawera Road. The Blue Lake is 8 km from the turn-off on SH30.

These two water-filled volcanic craters are obviously named for their colour and in Maori are known respectively as Tikitapu and Rotokakahi. On the northern shore of the Blue Lake is a sandy beach and a boat ramp adjoining a large picnic area. The track around the lake begins from the western side of this picnic area and is shaded by trees all the way, so this is a pleasant walk even on a hot day. The lake has no visible outlet, but drains underground into the Green Lake which is 20 metres lower. The water level rises and falls substantially from year to year – at times the lake is ringed by beautiful small beaches, while at other times all but two of the beaches disappear.

When you reach the car park at the opposite end of the lake, take some time to view the Green Lake and then return to the point where the track meets the car park. From here take the steps down to a lovely sheltered beach and then continue following the track around the shoreline where it eventually emerges a short distance from the starting point.

24 Hinehopu's Track   Easy   🚶   2 hours return

* ✳ A walk that combines lake scenery, native bush and history.
* ➤ At the eastern end of Lake Rotoiti, turn off SH30 into Tamatea Street and continue for 500 metres to the car park where the track begins. There is very limited car parking at the Lake Rotoehu end.

This well-formed track through attractive bush links Lakes Rotoiti and Rotoehu. There are three entrances, none of which is particularly well marked; the best starting point is at the Lake Rotoiti end. The highlight of the walk is the famous matai tree where, as a baby, Hinehopu was hidden from enemies by her mother. It was also under this tree that she met her husband Pikiao; many of the Ngati Pikiao iwi trace their lineage directly back to this couple. The tree is right by the main road, which does detract from the atmosphere somewhat.

It was also along this track that Nga Puhi warriors, led by Hongi Hika, launched their attack on Rotorua by dragging their waka along the track from Rotoehu to Rotoiti.

25 Te Koutu Pa   Easy   🚶   40 minutes return

* ✳ A walk to an historic pa site on the Eastern Okataina Walkway.
* ➤ At the car park by Lake Okataina at the end of Lake Okataina Road.

Te Koutu pa was the most important settlement on Lake Okataina, and easily defended on a small peninsula jutting out into the lake. The pa is noted for its stone kumara storage pits dug into the hillside and still visible today. The walk begins through the archway by the car park and follows the shoreline of the lake through the bush. Huge rocky bluffs soar above the track which continues all the way to Lake Tarawera.

26 Twin Craters/Ngahopua Track   Easy   🚶 40 minutes return

✳ A short walk through magnificent bush leads to a viewpoint over two small craters.

➤ Turn off SH30 at Lake Rotoiti into Lake Okataina Road. The walk begins 4 km on the left, opposite the turn-off to the Okataina Education Centre. Parking is limited and it is best to park on the road leading to the Education Centre.

A crater formed over 3000 years ago now holds two small lakes, Rotongata and Rotoatua. The track begins through a grove of spectacular large totara, though most of the trees along the track are tawa, their foliage giving the forest a soft filtered light. The steady climb leads to a high ridge overlooking the first lake, Rotongata, and then follows the ridge to a lookout over Rotoatua. There is no point going further than this as the lookout points beyond this are overgrown and the track quickly leads downhill from the lookout.

27 Kerosene Creek   Easy   🚶 10 minutes return

✳ A stream passes over hot rocks creating the perfect swimming hole.

➤ Kerosene Creek Road, on the right just past Rainbow Mountain Reserve. The hot stream is 2 km down this unsealed forestry road.

A popular swimming hole with locals, Kerosene Creek is a hot water stream, heated by the water of the creek passing over hot rocks. The temperature of the water varies considerably and you need to move up and down the creek to find a spot to suit. Particularly popular is the hot waterfall, great for a neck and back massage.

Note that this is a public reserve and as there is no knowing what might go in the water upstream it is best not to put your head underwater. Also it is relatively isolated and in recent years there have been considerable problems with cars being broken into.

28 Rainbow Mountain/Maungakakaramea

Easy 🚶 20 minutes return

✹ An active crater lake nestles below coloured cliffs.

➤ On SH30 south of Rotorua on the road to Waiotapu, 500 metres on the left past the Murupara/Waikaremoana turn-off.

A short walk up through manuka leads to a lookout over the bright green waters of the lake that now occupies the crater of Maungakakaramea. Still geothermally active, the lake presents a rare sight, with ducks swimming unperturbed at one end, while at the other the water furiously boils and steams. Above the lake tower the raw cliffs of multi-hued volcanic rocks that give this mountain its European name.

29 Craters of the Moon Easy 🚶 1 hour

✹ One of the most active and changeable thermal areas in New Zealand.

➤ 6 km north of Lake Taupo turn into Karapiti Road.

The Craters of the Moon, one of the most recent and most active thermal fields in the area, is constantly changing. Over the years the thermal areas have expanded considerably and the thermal activity is unpredictable: sometimes massive columns of steam rise from the entire area, while at other times it is disappointingly quiet. The most common thermal activity is steam vents, though there is one major crater with furiously boiling mud or water depending on the water levels. The area is open, with intriguing low-growing plants that have adapted to the inhospitable environment.

There is an entrance fee.

30 Huka Falls Walkway Easy 🚶 2 hours return

✹ The Waikato River is at its most pure as it exits from Lake Taupo, an iridescent blue-green colour which is then forced into a frothy mass over the Huka Falls.

➤ Either from Huka Falls or from Spa Park off Spa Road, Taupo.

The best way to start this walk is to begin from Spa Park in Taupo and preferably not visit Huka Falls beforehand. From Spa Park the track follows the river downstream from the point where a small hot water stream joins the river, creating a popular swimming hole where the hot water mingles with the cooler water of the Waikato River. The track then follows the southern bank of the river through a variety of vegetation, not all of it exactly pristine, but with extensive planting of native trees along the track this can only improve.

The river as it leaves Lake Taupo is just plain stunning. The swirling waters are clean and clear, and are a beautiful iridescent blue-green colour. The initially tranquil waters become increasingly swift as the falls near. The track is in excellent condition, though there are some steep parts, but this gives the walker the opportunity to look out over the luxurious Huka Lodge and the National Kayak Centre.

What visitors who go directly to the falls will not appreciate is just how big the river is at this stage, and just how much water is forced through the narrow gap at the falls themselves. The sheer volume of beautiful bright clear water that gushes through the narrow gap more than makes up for the modest size of these falls. Over 200,000 litres per second roar over the 3-metre falls with a fury that is truly impressive.

If you haven't organised someone to pick you up, you have to return the way you came; there is no return track on the other side of the river.

31 Motuoapa Lookout   Easy 🚶 15 minutes return

* A wide view over Lake Taupo from the south.

➤ The track is off SH1 at Motuoapa, right next to Motuoapa Lodge, about 10 km north of Turangi.

A short steep walk leads to a wooden platform that gives an excellent view over the marina at Motuoapa immediately below, and across Lake Taupo looking north. Beyond the wooden platform a rough track offers promise of a still better viewpoint, but don't bother: it only leads to a forestry road.

32 Thermal Tokaanu   Easy   𝕏   20 minutes

* Boiling mud and crystal-clear hot pools are hidden among the trees.

➤ The walk begins over the bridge and immediately to the right of the Tokaanu Thermal Pools off SH41 just north of Turangi.

Once used by local Maori for bathing and cooking, this active thermal area is a pleasant experience. Pools of crystal-clear water bubble up from deep in the earth, while in other places brilliant green-blue pools steam gently among the manuka. Small pots of boiling mud plop steadily, while elsewhere hissing steam escapes from fissures in the ground. Much of the short loop track is on boardwalks and most of it is safely fenced. When crossing the bridge by the pools, keep an eye out for the large trout swimming languidly in the clear water below.

33 Tongariro National Trout Centre   Easy   𝕏   30 minutes

* Trout can be seen in various stages of development in this pleasant riverside walk.

➤ SH1, 4 km south of Turangi.

Trout in the Taupo area are sustained by wild trout spawning in the rivers and lakes; while trout usually spend some time during their life at sea, in this area Lake Taupo acts as a substitute ocean. The hatchery at the National Trout Centre is a safeguard should a natural disaster seriously affect the fish numbers in the area. The complex raises trout from eggs and at all times of the year there are usually trout in some growth stage on show. The Visitor Centre has excellent displays on all aspects of the trout fishery including a fascinating collection of rods and flies.

A series of paths links the various pools and leads down to the Tongariro River, where an underground glass viewing chamber allows visitors to see the trout below water. The paths are a little confusing to follow, but it is impossible to get lost.

The Centre is open daily from 10 am to 4 pm from 1 December to 30 April, 10 am to 3 pm from 1 May to 30 November. A donation is appreciated.

34 Lake Rotopounamu   Easy 🚶 2 hours

✱ A small lake fringed by virgin native forest nestles in the lee of Mt Pihanga.

➤ Travelling on SH47 from Turangi, the track is located on the left on the downhill side of the Te Ponanga Saddle.

Mt Pihanga is the beautiful mountain that in Maori legend was fought over by Tongariro and Taranaki, and it is appropriate that this equally beautiful lake is located on the lower slopes of this mountain. The name means Greenstone Lake (referring to the colour of the water, as no greenstone is found here), though the water is not always green. From the road it is a short but steady climb up to the lake, which was formed thousands of years ago by a giant landslide and has no visible outlook. The track around the lake is largely flat, following the edge of the lake through mature forest of red beech, kahikatea, rimu and matai. On the eastern side of the lake is Long Beach, an ideal picnic spot and a good place for a swim on a hot summer's day.

35 Tongariro National Park: Taranaki Falls
Easy 🚶 1½ hours

✱ A walk through beech forest and volcanic landscapes to a dramatic waterfall in the shadow of Mt Ruapehu.

➤ The track starts in the small street behind the Chateau Tongariro, just below the Visitor Centre.

The walk to the Taranaki Falls is one of the best in the National Park for those on a day visit, as the loop walk traverses a wide range of terrain from the sub-alpine to beech forest, with excellent views of the volcanoes.

The lower section of the loop dips through tussock fields and follows a valley that has escaped the more recent lava flows and is dense with cool beech forest and ferns. The falls themselves burst through a narrow gap in an old lava flow and the water plunges 20 metres in a single fall over the cliff face. At the first entrance to the track, the current signage doesn't indicate that this is a loop track, and unfortunately many people return along this track after having viewed the falls. However, at the falls continue uphill to the left of the falls and return via the upper track. This area is more open and has a raw feel to it on account of having been subject to more recent lava flows, which are very obvious along this section of the track. Keep an eye out for tiny hebes, alpine daisies and other delicately flowering mountain plants.

36 Tongariro National Park: The Mounds
Easy ⅄ 15 minutes return

✳ Remnants of a giant landslide.

➤ Turn off SH47 towards Whakapapa Village. The track is marked to the right.

Not exactly a riveting view, The Mounds are, however, fascinating geologically. These hillocks were formed by a landslide of volcanic material down the northern slopes of Mt Ruapehu so massive that the debris created a wave pattern that resulted in a series of small mounds spread over a distance of many kilometres. There is a viewing platform on one of the higher mounds that gives a glimpse of the scale of this huge landslide.

37 Tongariro National Park: Tawhai Falls
Easy ⅄ 20 minutes return

✳ A rushing mountain stream drops into bush-fringed water.

➤ Turn off SH47 towards Whakapapa Village. The track is marked to the left.

Set in a narrow rocky valley lined with mountain beech, this very pretty small waterfall drops over the edge of an ancient lava flow and is easily accessible from the road.

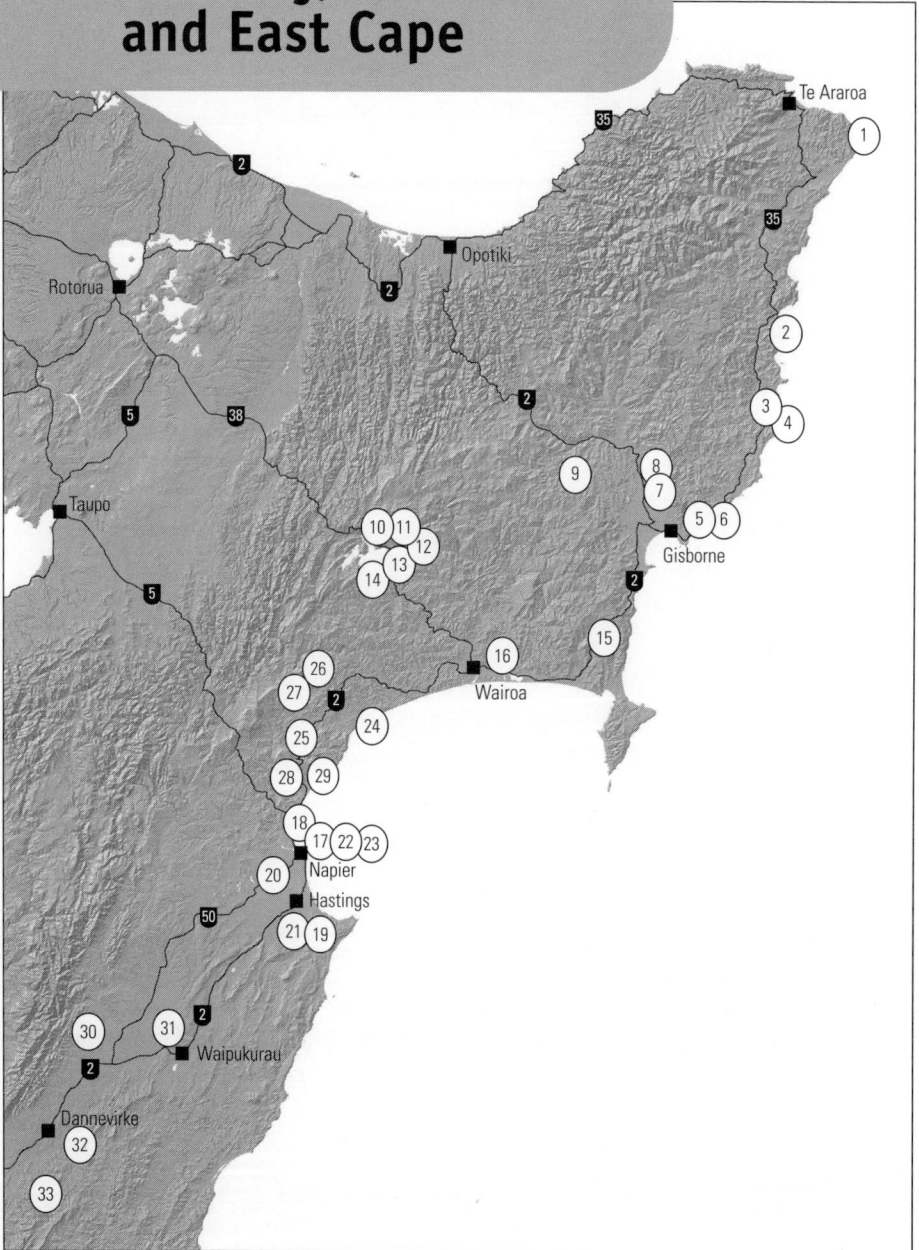

Hawke's Bay, Gisborne and East Cape

Te Araroa
1

35

35

Opotiki
2

Rotorua

2

5
38

Taupo

5

9

8
7

10 11
12
13
14

5 6
Gisborne
2

15

16
Wairoa

26
27
2

24

25

28 29

18
17 22 23
Napier
20
Hastings
50
21 19

30
31
2
Waipukurau

2
Dannevirke
32

33

1 East Cape Lighthouse Medium ⅄ 1 hour return

✳ An historic lighthouse towers above the easternmost point of the New Zealand mainland.

➤ 20 km from Te Araroa on an unsealed and winding road.

This lighthouse was originally built in 1900 on nearby East Island despite warnings from local Maori that the island was tapu. Continuous problems with access, landslides and earthquakes, including the death of four men by drowning during construction, finally convinced authorities to dismantle and move the lighthouse to its present site in 1922. The 150-metre climb is steep in places and includes a long flight of stairs.

2 Anaura Bay Medium

✳ Views over the stunning Anaura Bay and Motuoroi Island.

➤ 15 km north of Tolaga Bay turn off SH35 into Anaura Bay. At the beach turn left and follow the road to the camping ground. The track starts opposite the entrance to the camping ground.

⅄ Lookout: 25 minutes return

Loop walk: 1½ hours

The bush at Anaura Bay is much heralded as the finest and largest remaining coastal forest on the East Cape. However, whoever built the track did a very strange thing. Apart from a couple of short sections of no particular interest, the walkway determinedly avoids the bush altogether, and in fact the longest section of the track is through pine forest with other sections on the outside of the reserve looking in. Unless you really want to do the loop walk, save your energy and go for a walk on the beach, which is without a doubt one of the most beautiful on the East Cape.

The track to the lookout is worth the effort and winds steadily uphill through regenerating bush, along a small gully which contains a surprising number of native birds. At the top of the hill a short track to the left leads to the lookout over Anaura Bay and Motuoroi Island.

3 Tolaga Bay Wharf   Easy   入   30 minutes return

* ✳ The longest wharf in the Southern Hemisphere.

* ➤ South end of Tolaga Bay.

Built in 1929 at considerable expense and over 600 metres long, the Tolaga Bay wharf is an indication of the vital role that sea shipping played in the development of New Zealand. For much of New Zealand's early history, it was the sea that provided the link with the outside world. Wharves such as the one at Tolaga Bay were key to the success of the fledging agriculture industry: without sea access it was virtually impossible to get goods to market. With the advent of better roading, sea transport went rapidly into decline and all along the East Cape flourishing seaside communities such as Tokomaru Bay, Waipiro Bay, Hicks Bay and Te Araroa saw both their importance and their populations slowly dwindle.

4 Cooks Cove Walkway   Medium   入   50 minutes return to the lookout

* ✳ Views over Cooks Cove and Tolaga Bay.

* ➤ Wharf Road, signposted off SH35 at the southern end of Tolaga Bay.

Lieutenant James Cook's first landing, at the Turanganui River at modern-day Gisborne, was, through a series of misunderstandings, a disaster, resulting in the death of several Maori. In desperate need of water and firewood he sailed north to this cove in October 1769.

The walkway to the cove takes 2½ hours return, but this walk to the lookout is much shorter and has the best views. Mainly through open farmland, the easy uphill walk leads to a wooden platform that looks down on Cooks Cove below. Tolaga Bay is not visible from the lookout, but walk uphill to the left around the end of the fence to a grassy area, and from here there are fantastic views north over the bay. Watch your step, though, as this is the top of a steep cliff – don't go too close to the edge.

The track is closed for lambing from 1 August to Labour Weekend (last weekend in October).

5 Makorori Point, Wainui Beach   Easy 🚶 30 minutes return

* ✳ Coastal views over the splendid Makorori and Wainui beaches.

* ➤ The track is off SH35 at the north end of Wainui beach, Gisborne, just as the road climbs uphill.

Makorori Point lies between Wainui and Makorori beaches, and has spectacular coastal views to the south, beyond Young Nicks Head to the Mahia Peninsula, while to the north lies the magnificent and undeveloped Makorori Beach.

The initial section of the walk is up steep steps to a lookout point over Wainui beach. It then wanders along a wide grass track to a lookout point over Makorori Beach. There is a track down to the road from the Makorori end, but this means walking back along SH35 which is not a pleasant option as vehicles travel really fast and there is nowhere to walk off the road. It is also best to park down by the beach and walk the short distance up the hill to the start of the track as there is no parking at the beginning of the walk.

Just across the road and up the hill a little is Okitu Bush, a small coastal forest remnant with a loop track to a lookout that takes around 20 minutes.

6 Kaiti Hill, Gisborne   Medium

* ✳ Beginning from the historic Cook Memorial, the track leads uphill to wide views over the Gisborne district.

* ➤ Follow the road to the Port and Cook Memorial. The track starts opposite.

* 🚶 Cook Statue: 45 minutes return

  Te Kuri A Paoa lookout: 10 minutes return

A steady to steep uphill climb leads to a lookout over Gisborne city, with views inland and across Poverty Bay to Young Nicks Head (Te Kuri-a-Paoa). A little further along is the Cook statue. Erected in 1969 to commemorate the bicentenary of Cook's first landing in New Zealand, the bronze statue in fact bears no resemblance to James Cook. Furthermore, the uniform is Italian and not British. The statue was cast from a marble statue sold as James Cook in the 19th century to a gullible New Zealander by some sharp-talking Italian. Right alongside the statue is a pohutukawa tree planted by Diana, Princess of Wales, in 1983. From this point it will take another 20 minutes return to the car park lookout further uphill.

Hawke's Bay, Gisborne and East Cape

From the Te Kuri-a-Paoa lookout, there is a steep fitness trail that is shorter but all steps to the top, while the Shady Oaks track climbs much more gradually.

7 Gray's Bush Easy

✴ A beautiful tiny bush remnant with an unusual mixture of puriri and kahikatea.

➤ 10 km from Gisborne on the Back Ormond Road.

🚶 Short loop: 20 minutes
Long loop: 40 minutes

The only remaining lowland bush on the Poverty Bay plain, Gray's Bush is an impressive subtropical forest with massive kahikatea and puriri and a dense understorey of nikau palms. The combination of kahikatea and puriri is unusual, in that the puriri tend to favour well-drained soils while kahikatea thrive in wet conditions. Early recognition of this unique forest combination saved this bush from being felled. Furthermore, the height of the kahikatea has resulted in the puriri growing much taller and straighter than their usual spreading habit.

The tracks are not clearly marked, but the reserve is so small that it is impossible to get lost.

8 Waihirere Domain Easy 🚶 45 minutes

✴ A very pleasant walk along a pretty stream to a small waterfall.

➤ 12 km from Gisborne on the Back Ormond Road, turn into Waihirere Domain Road.

A popular picnic spot, the Waihirere Domain has a large grassed area with tables, and a playground and toilet facilities. The walk begins over a small footbridge and continues along a tree-shaded valley to a small waterfall with a pool suitable for swimming.

9 Eastwoodhill Arboretum Easy 🚶 At least 2 hours

✳ The most impressive collection of Northern Hemisphere trees in New Zealand.

➤ Wharekopae Road, Ngatapa, 35 km from Gisborne. From the city take SH2 south. At the large roundabout just over the Waipaoa River turn right and after 50 metres turn left and follow the signs.

Eastwoodhill was the life work of the eccentric William Cook, who began planting trees on his farm when he returned from Europe after the First World War. With the idea that native trees did not do well in the Poverty Bay back country, Cook spent the next half-century until his death in 1967 planting more than 4000 exotic trees and shrubs. Today, Cook's collection of trees is unique in the Southern Hemisphere, and the 150-hectare property is a maze of gardens and paths. While autumn attracts the most visitors, there is plenty to see in every season. Now a Garden of National Significance, Eastwoodhill is open daily 9 am to 5 pm and there is an entry fee (for more information see www.eastwoodhill.org.nz).

10 Waikaremoana: Papakorito Falls Easy 🚶 10 minutes return

✳ An easy walk to a very pretty waterfall.

➤ 1.2 km down Aniwaniwa Road opposite the Aniwaniwa Visitor Centre.

Papakorito is a very picturesque waterfall that drops over a wide bluff and fans out over a rocky outcrop into a broad pool. The nearby Visitor Centre is well worth a visit. Not only does it have excellent displays of both Tuhoe and natural history, it is also home to the Colin McCahon mural *Urewera*, painted in 1975 and dramatically stolen in 1997 (it was returned 15 months later).

11 Waikaremoana: Whatapo Bay Easy 🚶 15 minutes return

✳ A sandy swimming beach with views across the lake.

➤ 6 km south of the Aniwaniwa Visitor Centre.

A short track leads down to a pleasant sandy beach backed by bush and with views out over the lake and south to Panekiri Bluff. It's a good swimming spot if you are game enough to brave the cool waters of the lake. In the car park is an enclosure containing kaka beak, an attractive native flowering shrub that is now rare in the wild owing to introduced pests such as possums.

12 Waikaremoana: Lou's Lookout   Medium 🚶 45 minutes return

* ✱ Wend your way through limestone caves and boulders to fantastic lake views.
* ➤ 8.5 km south of the Aniwaniwa Visitor Centre.

A steady, but not hard, uphill walk, this track weaves through massive limestone boulders that are a startling indication of the size of the landslip that occurred over 2000 years ago, blocking the Waikaretaheke River and forming Lake Waikaremoana. The boulders now form arches, caves and overhangs along this track. At the top the reward is a fantastic lake view that includes the dramatic Panekiri Bluff to the south. The lookout is named after Tuai policeman Lou Dolman, who helped build the tracks around the lake in the 1960s.

13 Waikaremoana: Lake Kiriopukae   Easy 🚶 40 minutes return

* ✱ A tiny lake reminiscent of a Japanese garden.
* ➤ The track is at the beginning of the Lake Waikaremoana Great Walk at Onepoto, 12 km south of the Aniwaniwa Visitor Centre.

More pond than lake, Kiriopukae lies in a wetland that expands and shrinks considerably with the seasons. Weathered limestone outcrops and boulders are scattered around the lake, giving the appearance of being carefully placed, creating the distinctive atmosphere of a Japanese garden.

To reach the lake follow the first 500 metres of the Great Lake Walk to the flat grassed area, and then take the track to the left which leads downhill to the lake. This flat area was once the parade ground for the Armed Constabulary Redoubt but very little remains apart from an old historic cemetery (to the right of the lake and hard to find), and a limestone rock poignantly carved with the names and dates of soldiers stationed here in the 1860s and '70s.

14 Waikaremoana: Panekiri Bluff, First Trig

Medium ⚐ 2 hours return

✳ Dramatic views over Lake Waikaremoana.

➤ This is the first section of the Lake Waikaremoana Great Walk from Onepoto, 12 km south of the Aniwaniwa Visitor Centre.

For those visiting Waikaremoana, and for whom the Great Walk (5 to 7 days) is not an option, this short walk will give a taste of one of the better-known sections of the walk. The massive bulk of the Panekiri Bluff dominates the southern end of the lake, rising to over 1100 metres at the summit known as Puketapu (5 hours one way). However, the more modest first trig point can be reached after a steady uphill walk of 1 hour and has magnificent views over the lake. The track begins at the far end of the flat grassed area that was the old parade ground.

Other lake sections of the walk can be reached by water taxi. The Visitors Centre will have up-to-date information on this.

15 Morere Springs Scenic Reserve Easy ⚐ 30 minutes

✳ Natural hot springs in a stunning nikau forest.

➤ At Morere on SH2, just north of Nuhaka and 60 km south of Gisborne.

These hot springs are set in the 364-hectare Morere Springs Scenic Reserve, which has a number of tracks ranging from 30 minutes to 3 hours, and is particular famous for the luxuriant growth of the nikau palms. The springs, producing 250,000 litres of hot water a day, are especially unusual in that they tap into mineral water that is actually ancient sea water, even though Morere is situated inland from the ocean.

The loop walk is almost entirely through dense groves of nikau palm with huge fronds, giving this reserve an unexpected tropical feel. Other trees include rimu, totara, matai, tawa, kohekohe and pukatea, with a dense understorey of ferns, mosses and vines. There are a number of pools indoor and out, both for families and for those wanting a more relaxed soak, though the water temperature is more warm than hot. There is an entrance fee to the pools.

16 Waiatai Reserve Easy 🚶 20 minutes return

✳ A massive puka tree reputed to be the largest in the country.

➤ SH2, 4 km east of Wairoa.

The size of the puka tree will come as a surprise to those who consider this tree suitable for a small city garden. Believed to be the largest puka in New Zealand and standing 10 metres tall, this broad multi-branched tree has much smaller leaves in the mature form than the more familiar wide leaves of the young tree. The track to the tree is not well marked and is overgrown, but the reserve is very small and it is impossible to get lost. After crossing the stile, follow the fence-line up the hill to some steps which lead to an indistinct track. The puka is not marked but is located in a small clearing with a picnic table.

17 Napier Botanical Gardens and Historic Cemetery
Easy 🚶 1 hour

✳ One of New Zealand's oldest public gardens and an historic cemetery.

➤ Spencer Road, off Chaucer Road South, Napier.

Located in a deep gully on Bluff Hill, these hidden gardens were established as early as 1855. Several massive specimen trees still stand from this period and would easily count as the best examples of their type in New Zealand. In addition to these superb trees, there are formal gardens and a number of theme gardens, including a subtropical garden with palms and cycads.

Start the walk at the entrance to the gardens on Spencer Road and slowly wind your way uphill to the top gates. Turn right immediately and enter the old Napier Cemetery, which dates from 1854 and includes the graves of early missionaries William Colenso and Bishop William Williams. In keeping with the custom of the time, most of the gravestones are large and elaborate, but there are also a number of very rare wooden memorials dating from the 1860s. As was typical of the period, the cemetery is carefully laid out by religious denomination. Appropriately enough the cemetery is hard to get out of, with the lower exits blocked off, but return uphill a little way and follow the stalag-like fence between the cemetery and the gardens and this path will take you back to Spencer Road.

18 Whakamaharatanga Walkway Easy

✳ This ancient pa site gives an excellent view over the Ahuriri Estuary.

➤ Take SH22 north from Napier. Just before Bay View turn left into Onehunga Road. The walk begins 1 km on the left down this road.

𝕏 Rorookuri Hill Summit: 25 minutes return

Otiere pa and hill summit: 45 minutes

Circular track: 1 hour

Rorookuri Hill was once an island in the Ahuriri Lagoon, which occupied the area between the hill and Napier. Rising over 1 metre in the 1931 earthquake much of the lagoon became dry land, and subsequent drainage for farming and airport development reduced the wetland further still. Now only a small tidal lagoon remains just south of the airfield. The pa sites on this hill were key to the control of the lagoon's important food resources, and their strategic location is obvious, with views along the bay both north and south. Now farmland, the walkway is closed for lambing during July, August and September.

19 Maraetotara Falls Heritage Walk Easy 𝕏 20 minutes return

✳ A great swimming hole and the remains of an old power station.

➤ Take the Waimarama Road off SH2 south of Napier out towards Ocean Beach. After the road leaves the Tukituki River, Maraetotara Road turns off to the right. The entrance to the falls is 2.5 km down this road and clearly marked by the white painted fencing.

The falls are actually a concrete weir built in 1922 by the Havelock Borough Council on top of the existing falls to provide water for a small power station downstream. The power station is long gone, and today large trees shade the crystal-clear waters of the Maraetotara River making this short walk particularly appealing. Below the falls is a large deep swimming hole, very popular in summer, complete with a rope swing to drop swimmers deep into the cool waters.

While the walk is easy, at one point there is a stainless steel ladder down the side of the weir that needs a bit of careful negotiation.

20 Otatara Pa Historic Reserve Medium 🚶 1 hour return

✳ Two of Hawke's Bay's most ancient and important pa sites on a high hill above the Tutaekuri River.

➤ Springfield Road, off Gloucester Street where it crosses the Tutaekuri River.

The location alone of Otatara pa would indicate its importance. Situated high above the Tutaekuri River, the views from Hikurangi pa at the top of the hill are superb and encompass all of the Heretaunga Plain and far inland. The two pa have been occupied since 1400. In earlier times the pa alongside the river was further protected by a lagoon which disappeared in the 1931 earthquake (see page 113).

The recent addition of a carved gateway, palisades and pou gives the reserve an ancient air and the open grassy site allows a clear view of terraces, defensive ditches, house sites and kumara pits.

21 Te Mata Peak Medium 🚶 1 hour return

✳ Fantastic views from the peak of the rugged Te Mata Range.

➤ Te Mata Peak Road, Havelock North.

The rugged barren peak of Te Mata, rising nearly 400 metres above the Tukituki Valley, has the most spectacular view in every direction, from Mahia (to the north-east) through to Ruapehu (north-west) on a fine day. In Maori legend the range is the body of a giant who died trying to eat his way through the ridge between the Heretaunga Plain and the Tukituki River.

While a road goes to the peak and it is easy to drive to the top, it is worth spending some time walking here in order to gain a better appreciation of this wonderful countryside with views in every direction. The hills are laced with a network of tracks so it pays to check out the information board at the entrance to the park. Make sure you identify the mountain-bike-only track as you will be flattened for sure walking on this.

An easy walk begins at the second car park just past the restaurant. This steady uphill follows the rocky escarpment overlooking the Tukituki River to Te Mata Peak at 399 metres. From this point you can return down the road or continue past the main car park and along the ridge to the Redwood Grove and then return via the Te Mata Walk.

Above Mt Maunganui/Mauao. The base track around Mauao links the sheltered Tauranga Harbour to one of New Zealand's most famous surf beaches. Several tracks also lead to the summit, from which the views on a fine day are well worth the effort.

Below Otarawairere Beach, Ohope Beach. Fringed by old pohutukawa, this beach is accessible only on foot. It's just a short distance from Ohope Beach and part of the 17-km Nga Tapuwae O Toi Walk.

Above Historic Whakatane River. The intricately carved gateway to Muriwai's Cave, a site that was once highly tapu (sacred).

Right The Redwoods, Whakarewarewa Forest, Rotorua. Planted as an early forestry experiment and now over a century old, these trees make for a pleasant shady walk on a hot day.

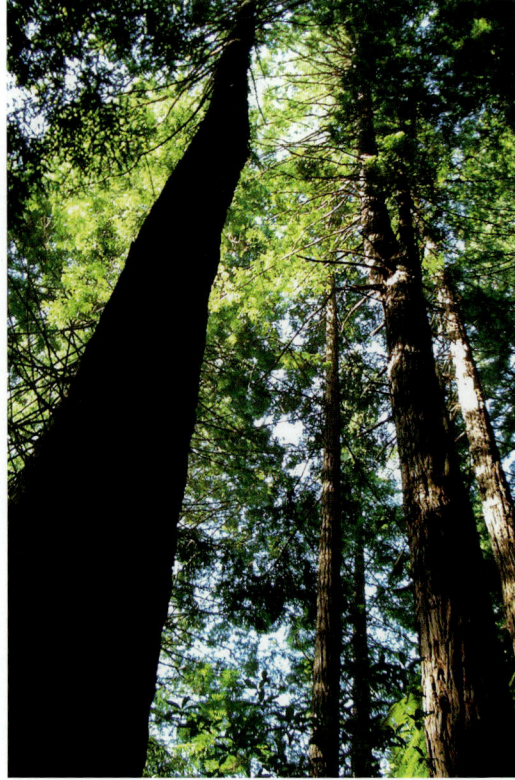

Below Okareka Walkway Rotorua. This hide, accessed by boardwalks through wetland fringing Lake Okareka, is an ideal place to spot aquatic birds such as pukeko, ducks and shags.

Left Craters of the Moon, Taupo. One of the Volcanic Plateau's most active geothermal fields, this area changes from year to year. The steam is particularly good on a wet day or after heavy rain.

Below Huka Falls, Taupo. The Waikato River is forced through a narrow rock channel, creating a thrilling rush of water.

Above Tokaanu Thermal Walk, Turangi. Located next to the thermal swimming pools, this walk has the most stunning pools of boiling hot water ranging from shimmering blues and greens to water so clear it appears non-existent.

Below Maraetotara Falls, Hawke's Bay. A weir sits atop a small waterfall of beautiful clear water, making this the perfect spot for cooling off on a hot summer's day.

Above Three Sisters and Elephant Rock, Taranaki. Accessible only at low tide, two of the sisters still stand tall, while the third, worn away by the elements, is just a few metres high.

Left Mt Damper Falls, Taranaki. The highest single-drop waterfall in the North Island.

Below Te Henui Walkway, New Plymouth. In Te Henui cemetery, the elegant tomb of Mohammed Islam Salaman will cause walkers to think they have really wandered off-track.

Above Lake Kiriopukae, Te Urewera National Park.

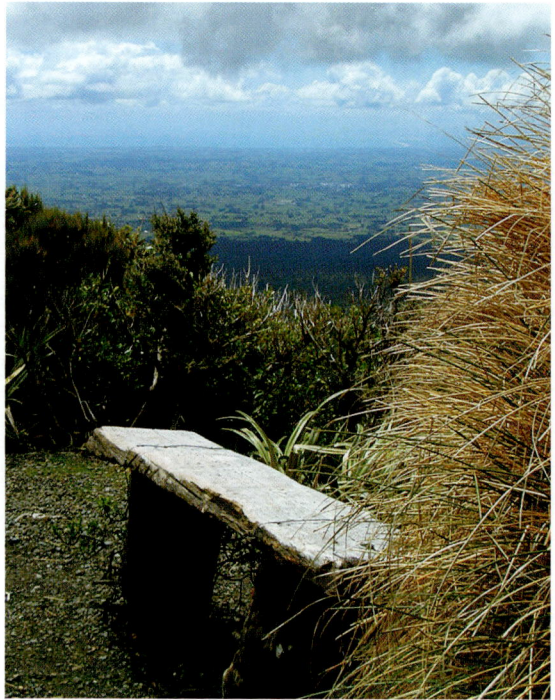

Right Holly Hut Track Lookout, Taranaki. This lookout above the treeline has superb views over New Plymouth and northern Taranaki.

Below Historic Wanganui City. Built of timber in 1899, the Opera House is just one of the many well-preserved historic buildings in central Wanganui, harking back to the heyday of the city as a major river port.

Above Cape Palliser Lighthouse, Wairarapa. The 278 steps lead straight up to a wide view along the wild coast. The nearby seal colony (below left) can be seen from the road.

Right Korokoro Dam Walk, Hutt Valley. This elegant concrete dam was built in 1903 to provide homes in Petone with clean drinking water.

Above Wellington Waterfront. The charming Clyde Quay boat sheds are just one highlight among many on this walk from Oriental Bay to the Wellington Railway Station.

Below Otari–Wilton's Bush, Wellington. At the entrance to one of New Zealand's most important collections of New Zealand plants, this carved gateway begins a walkway that crosses a steep gully through the tops of native trees.

22 Art Deco Napier Easy 🚶 1 hour

✳ Well-preserved art deco style buildings that rank with the best in the world.

➤ Begin the walk at Napier's Deco Centre, 163 Tennyson Street.

On 3 February 1931 a massive earthquake hit the Hawke's Bay region, causing widespread damage from Wairoa in the north to Dannevirke in the south, killing 258 people and devastating the small cities of Hastings and Napier. Napier city suffered particularly badly when fire broke out in the central business area following the quake. Large sections of Bluff Hill collapsed and the surrounding lagoons all but disappeared when the land rose over 2 metres. The city was rebuilt in what was then the most fashionable of styles – art deco, Spanish mission and stripped classic – and as all the new buildings had to be low level and built in concrete, the resulting effect is surprisingly uniform and appealing.

The area containing most of the art deco buildings is compact, and concentrated on Tennyson, Hastings, Emerson and Herschell Streets and Marine Parade. Key buildings include the Scinde Building, the Daily Telegraph Building, the State Insurance Building, the Bank of New South Wales, the Masonic Hotel, the Colonade, the Soundshell, ASB Bank and the shop façades on Emerson Street.

Art Deco Weekend, one of Hawke's Bay's most popular events, celebrates the 1930s lifestyle. Held over a three-day period on the third weekend in February, the festival includes more than 80 events ranging from picnics and themed dinners through to jazz concerts, and culminates in a huge street parade through Napier on the Saturday.

Just to the south of the city centre is Clive Square, noted for its formal flower beds, huge Moreton Bay fig tree and immensely tall Washingtonia palms. Set out as a garden in 1884, the square became the temporary Napier shopping centre after the 1931 earthquake and was affectionately known as Tin Town.

23 Napier: Marine Parade   Easy 🚶 1 hour

* A combination of history and seaside attractions.

➤ Start the walk at the junction of Coote Road and Marine Parade.

Built on rubble from the 1931 earthquake, the reserve on Marine Parade embodies an earlier age when promenading by the sea was a popular recreational activity. A few years ago this area had become shabby, but recent improvements have restored its former glory, and now formal gardens link the various attractions such as the Soundshell, swimming pool and skating rink. In particular, new paths and cycleways along the length of the foreshore have proved especially popular with locals and visitors alike. Unfortunately the beach along the waterfront is not very attractive for swimming, being both dangerous and mainly shingle.

Highlights along the Parade from north to south are as follows:

- Napier Prison, at 55 Coote Road off the northern end of the Parade, was opened in 1862 with 25 male and 24 female inmates including lunatics, alcoholics, children and dispossessed Maori. Life was hard and the prison regime included hard labour in the quarry opposite, now the Centennial Gardens. New Zealand's oldest prison, the current building is still largely in original condition and includes the solitary confinement cells, the hanging yard with a public gallery, a small graveyard, and cells complete with original bunks. Finally closed in 1993, the prison is now a popular backpackers complete with regular ghost sightings! Tours are conducted daily. The prison was also the setting for the reality television show *Redemption Hill*.

- Ocean Spa. A great outdoor swimming complex overlooking the sea, complete with a heated lap pool, spa and family pools as well as a steam room, sauna and café.

- Pania of the Reef. Aotearoa's very own Little Mermaid story, Pania left her sea people to be with her human, land-dwelling lover Karitoki. However, Pania's desire to see her family became too strong and when she decided to visit them for the very last time, her family trapped her in a cave below the sea where Pania became a reef with her arms forever reaching out for Karitoki. When the statue of Pania was stolen in 2005, the overwhelming affection of the local people for the statue was evident and she was soon restored, with great ceremony and relief, to her position on the waterfront.

- The Colonade is an Italianate structure built as a memorial to the earthquake victims. It features the bell from the HMS *Veronica*, which was anchored at Napier at the time of the earthquake and whose seamen were vital in the rescue efforts immediately following the quake.

- The Soundshell was built in art deco style in the 1930s. It is a popular spot for performances of all types, especially during the Art Deco Weekend.

- The National Aquarium of New Zealand is much further down the Parade, but worth the walk as this superb aquarium has the largest collection of marine and freshwater fish in the country. The aquarium is in two parts: the first is a tour through different parts of the world, while the second has a tunnel through a huge fish tank giving an excellent 'underwater' view of the fish. The scary animals are all here: crocodiles, sharks and piranha, along with the piranha's vegetarian cousin, the gentle paku. As well as fish, the complex has a walk-through kiwi house, and reptiles including tuatara.

24 Waikare Beach   Easy 🔥 40 minutes return

✳ A long sandy beach backed by huge cliffs battered by weather and earthquakes.

➤ At Putorino, 60 km north of Napier on SH2, turn into Waikare Road. Follow this narrow and unsealed road for 13 km to a camping ground by the river at the end of the road. The track begins at the far end of the small camping area.

From the camping area the track wanders up the hillside then follows the Waikare River down to the beach. The beach was once the main highway down the coast both in pre-European times for Maori, and for Pakeha prior to the road being built. The flat farmland on the other side of the river was the location of an early whaling station. The wide and wild beach is backed by huge crumbling cliffs, and clearly visible to the south is the massive Moeangiangi Slip, created when a 3 km section of the cliffs collapsed during the 1931 earthquake.

25 Lake Tutira Wildlife Refuge and Country Park Easy

✳ Waterbirds abound on this lake that was once part of the famous Tutira Station.

➤ On SH2, 44 km north of Napier.

🚶 Lake Waikopiro Walk: 20 minutes

Kahikanui and Galbraith Tracks: 1½ hours

This popular swimming and picnic spot was originally part of the Tutira Station owned by the farmer and author Herbert Guthrie-Smith. Very early on Guthrie-Smith recognised the need for conservation of native plants and birds, and in 1921 published his massive book, *Tutira: The story of a New Zealand sheep station*, based on years of painstaking observation and note-taking. The picnic area at the southern end of the lake was the site of the station's woolshed, and is now the beginning of several tracks in the Tutira Country Park. This area also was the site of a major pa, protected on two sides by the lakes and by a man-made moat on the other sides, though nothing now remains.

The lake is alive with waterbirds including duck, pukeko, swan, heron and teal, and the early richness of the area is attested to by numerous pa sites around the lake.

Adjoining Lake Tutira to the south is tiny Lake Waikopiro. The Kahikanui and Galbraith tracks form a loop on the eastern side of the lake; this walk begins at the very far end of the picnic area. This walk has views over the lake, crosses through regenerating native bush and takes in an old pa on a headland.

26 Shine Falls Easy 🚶 1½ hours return

✳ The highest waterfall in Hawke's Bay, located in a 'mainland island'.

➤ At the Tutira Store on SH2, 45 km north of Napier, turn into Matahorua Road. At the junction with Pohokura Road veer to the right (this is still Matahorua Road). After 5 km veer to the left into Heays Access Road. The beginning of the track is on the left, 7 km down this road.

Imagine a picture-perfect waterfall, with water tumbling down a rocky face into a large swimming hole, surrounded by native bush alive with birds, and you have the Shine Falls. At 58 metres this is the highest waterfall in Hawke's

Bay, and certainly one of the most attractive in the North Island with two streams breaking into myriad rivulets spreading down over a broad rock face into a wide and deep pool.

The falls are located in an 800-hectare 'mainland island', an area where predators are intensively controlled resulting in an obvious recovery of both bird and plant life in the reserve, where recently both kokako and kiwi have been reintroduced.

The first section of the track leads through farmland along a limestone gorge with rocky bluffs towering above the stream. The second section is through recovering bush, the floor of the forest thick with regenerating seedlings; and unlike so much of New Zealand forest, the bird life is conspicuous by its presence. The sudden appearance of the waterfall at the very end of the track increases the appeal of the walk.

It's a bit of journey to get to Shine Falls, and much of the road from Tutira is winding and gravel, but it is worth the effort.

27 Opouahi Lake   Easy   🚶 30 minutes return

✴ A short walk around a beautiful small bush-fringed lake.

➤ At the Tutira Store on SH2 45 km north of Napier, turn into Matahorua Road. At the junction with Pohokura Road turn left. The reserve is on the right, 4 km from the junction.

This delightful small lake is one of the few intact wetlands in Hawke's Bay. It supports a wide range of both bush and aquatic birdlife, including the rare spotless crake and brown kiwi. Formed by a massive landslip in times long gone, the small lake is surprising deep at 24 metres and is ringed by attractive bush including some fine old kowhai trees leaning out over the water. The track is well formed and flat all the way, and a small jetty gives access to the lake for kayakers and swimmers.

The lake is not well signposted from the road, so keep your eyes peeled as it is easy to miss.

28 Te Ana and Tangoio Falls Easy

✳ Two waterfalls in the Tangoio Falls Scenic Reserve.

➤ Well signposted on SH2, 27 km north of Napier.

🚶 Te Ana Falls: 30 minutes return

Tangoio Falls: 1 hour return

This 550-hectare bush reserve contains two attractive waterfalls, both very different. The Te Ana Falls plunge out of a gap in a rock face and into a small swimming hole, while the Tangoio Falls spread gracefully over a wide rock face in a fern- and moss-clad basin.

There is no signage indicating the track at the start of the walk, but cross the small bridge by the car park, head right past the picnic tables, and the wide track is obvious. A bit muddy in places, the gentle track leads through bush following the Kareaara Stream, first to the Te Ana Falls, at which point the track to the Tangoio Falls leads off the right. The track to the Tangoio Falls is a bit rougher and muddier than the first half of the track.

29 Waipatiki Reserve Medium 🚶 1¼ hours

✳ A lowland nikau forest near sandy Waipatiki Beach.

➤ From Napier take SH2 for 20 km then turn right into Tangoio Road (follow the signposts for Waipatiki Beach). After 6 km turn into Waipatiki Road. The reserve is clearly marked to the left.

The track initially plunges into lush bush festooned with mosses and thick with nikau palms, a startling contrast to the pine forest and bare tawny hills that surround the reserve. So striking is the subtropical nature of this reserve that many suppose this bush to be unusual, but what this bush makes so glaringly obvious is the harsh reality of how little lowland bush remains in the whole of the North Island from East Cape to Cape Palliser. The typical picture of the east coast is now one of steep grass-covered hill country, burnt brown in summer and scarred by numerous slips, and it is hard to believe that it was once densely covered by thick, lush native forest. Even here at the Waipatiki Reserve, with its dense nikau groves, the evidence of past logging is obvious with the scarcity of large trees and the presence of enormous stumps.

The initial part of the track is a steep uphill climb to a junction with a sign referring to an 'upper' and 'lower' track, but it doesn't matter which route you take as this part of the track is a loop. If you want to do the steep bit first, take the upper track.

It is worthwhile taking some time to visit the very attractive sandy Waipatiki Beach, which is just a few kilometres down the road at the bottom of the valley.

30 Monckton Scenic Reserve Easy 🚶 1 hour

* ✳ A beautiful small bush remnant with an appealing picnic area.

* ➤ Take SH50 north from the junction with SH2 between Dannevirke and Waipukurau. After 5 km turn left into Ashley Clinton Road. The reserve is on the right, 4.5 km down this road.

Apart from small reserves, lowland forest has long vanished from Hawke's Bay, making reserves such as this (just 17 hectares in size) very precious. A figure-of-eight loop walk winds through virgin bush dominated by kahikatea. The Tangarewai Stream passes through the reserve, and in parts is deeply shaded by the thick bush on either bank. There is an excellent picnic area with tables, shade trees and toilets.

31 Lindsay Scenic Reserve Easy 🚶 25 minutes

* ✳ A remnant of lowland bush alongside the pretty Tukituki River.

* ➤ After crossing the Tukituki River heading north from Waipukurau town on SH2, turn left into Lindsay Road, and after 2 km turn left into Scenic Road. At the stopbank turn right and park by the picnic area on the left by the river.

Although the tracks are not well marked it is impossible to get lost in this small bush reserve alongside the Tukituki River. Kahikatea dominate the treescape, and this bush contains some very impressive specimens of New Zealand's tallest tree. There is easy access to the river here; although it's not really deep enough to swim in during summer, it is a pleasant spot to cool off on a hot day.

32 Mangatoro Scenic Reserve Easy 𝕏 30 minutes

* A fine stand of totara and kahikatea along the Mangatoro Stream.

➤ From Dannevirke take the road east signposted Weber. After 11 km turn into Ngapaeruru Road; the reserve is on the right.

This loop walk through the 8-hectare reserve alongside the Mangatoro Stream passes through some fine tall kahikatea, rimu and matai, and one especially impressive totara tree. One section of the track is covered in a huge swathe of moss that is deep and cool to look at but surprisingly dry to the touch. The stream is ideal for a swim on a hot summer's day, and although the track is short there are some rough and muddy patches.

33 Waihi Falls Easy 𝕏 10 minutes return

* A picturesque waterfall drops into a swimming hole.

➤ From Dannevirke take the Weber road for 30 km, then turn right into Oporae Road for a further 12 km to the short Waihi Falls Road on the left. A substantial section of Oporae Road is unsealed.

Public appreciation of these falls as a local attraction was recognised very early on, and in 1899 this was the first scenic reserve established in Hawke's Bay. The Waihi River cascades 25 metres over a wide bluff into a large pool and the falls are especially spectacular after heavy rain. From the car park and picnic area the track is a short downhill walk through thin native bush that nonetheless contains some handsome old kowhai trees leading to a grassy area by the falls.

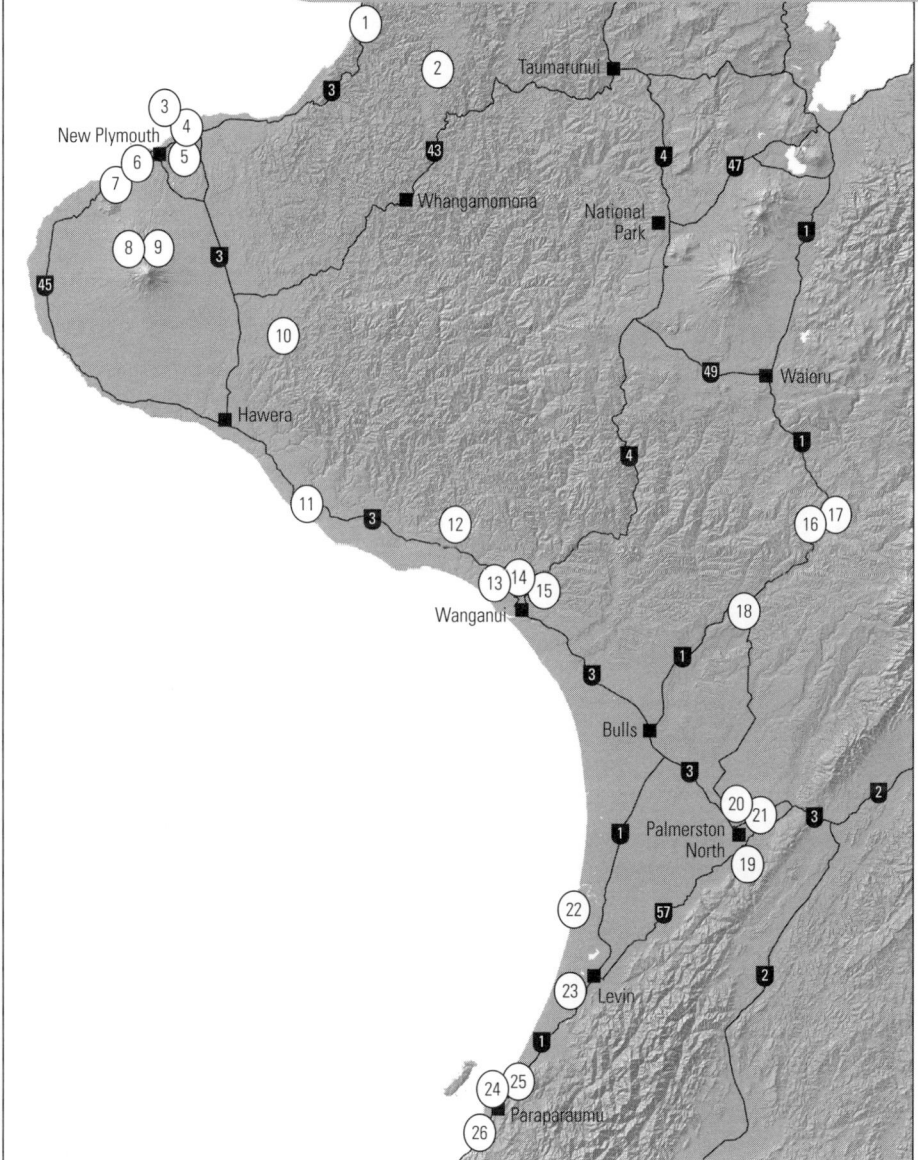

Taranaki, Wanganui and Manawatu

① Taumarunui

New Plymouth
③
④
⑥
⑦
⑤
⑧ ⑨
㊺
②
③
㊸
⑩
Whangamomona
National Park
④
㊼
①
Hawera
⑪
③
⑫
㊾
Waiouru
④
①
⑬⑭
⑮
Wanganui
⑯ ⑰
⑱
③
Bulls
③
①
⑳ ㉑
Palmerston North
⑲
③
②
⑳㉒
㊶
②
㉓ Levin
①
㉔ ㉕
Paraparaumu
㉖

121

1 Three Sisters and Elephant Rock   Easy   🚶   30 minutes return

* ✱ Offshore rock stacks set among dramatic coastal scenery.

* ➤ Clifton Road at the Tongaporutu River mouth, just south of Mokau.

The Three Sisters are tall rock remnants just offshore near the mouth of the Tongaporutu River. They are now nicknamed by locals the 'two and a half sisters': two of the sisters are around 25 metres high while the third sister is merely a few metres high, worn away by wind and waves (a century ago there was yet a fourth sister). Nearby is Elephant Rock which, as you guessed, looks like an elephant. In addition to the sisters, there are several large caves and rock arches, one of which contains curious rock carvings of indeterminate origin.

The views along this rugged wave-worn coast are dramatic, with Taranaki looming to the south and offshore oil platforms just visible. However, the beach here is accessible only close to low tide (best on an outgoing tide), and even then you will get your feet wet.

2 Mt Damper Falls   Easy   🚶   45 minutes return

* ✱ The highest single waterfall in the North Island.

* ➤ Moki Road, 16 km from the Whangamomona road, or follow the signs for 12 km from SH3 just south of Mokau.

At the Mt Damper Falls, a tributary of the Tongoporutu River plunges 74 metres in a single fall over a sheer cliff into a pool far below. The lookout point gives an excellent view high above the falls, but there is no access to the pool. A local story tells of the discovery of the falls by a local sheep farmer who lost his prize sheepdog after it was dragged over the cliff by a wild boar.

Part of the track is through farmland, while closer to the falls the track enters pleasant bush. The track is rough and muddy so make sure you wear old shoes.

3 Te Henui Walkway   Easy 人 1½ hours return to the Cumberland Bridge

* A combination of mature native and exotic trees along a clear rocky stream.

➤ While there are several entry points, the simplest for visitors is from New Plymouth's East End Reserve, off the Coastal Walkway.

This deep, almost secret valley cuts across the city from the coast and is typical of the rocky streams that slice through this old volcanic landscape. The walk follows the stream though a mixture of mature native trees, formal landscaped gardens and exotic trees. The valley shelters the track from the wind, and the trees lend a cool atmosphere to the easy walk. When you reach the Cumberland Street bridge you can either return the way you came or attempt the track on the south side of the stream, which is accessed immediately to the right of the bridge. This section of the walk is less developed and the signposting is erratic, which can be very confusing for a visitor. It does, however, feature the historic Te Henui Cemetery with the graves of early settlers and soldiers, and the spectacular mosque-like Mohammed Islam Salaman tomb.

The Te Henui walkway is a good alternative if the weather is too rough for the waterfront walk.

4 New Plymouth Coastal Walkway   Easy 人 1½ hours one way

* An excellent walkway along New Plymouth's waterfront.

➤ Accessible at any point along the city's coastal line.

New Plymouth has done a magnificent job in making its entire coastline accessible to the public. This walkway is so popular that at times it has the feel of a pedestrian motorway, as walkers jostle with joggers, prams, skateboarders, rollerbladers and cyclists. Covering 7 km from the port to the estuary of the Waiwhakaiho River, the walk has coastal views, city beaches, boulder-strewn banks, sand dunes and the sheltered Lake Rotomanu at the northern end near the river. A highlight of the walk is Len Lye's *Windwand*: 45 metres high, made of carbon fibre and glass, it is designed to sway dramatically in the wind. The section of the walk north of the city is the more interesting section.

The coastline is exposed to strong prevailing winds; if the wind becomes too much, an alternative is to return via the more sheltered streets. Most people access the walkway from the city centre where parking can be problematic.

As an alternative, begin the walk at one of the several access points north of the city with much easier (and free) parking.

5 Pukekura Park   Easy 🚶 At least 1 hour

✳ One of New Zealand's finest public parks.

➤ Main entrance at the top of Liardet Street, New Plymouth.

Established in 1876 and later expanded, Pukekura Park and Brooklands now cover 52 hectares. While most people are content to just stroll around the small lake, this park is well worth further exploring.

Fifteen hectares of what was then a swampy valley was set aside as a public park in 1876, and was at first known as the Recreation Ground. In 1934, a farm known as Brooklands was added to the park, and the famous Bowl of Brooklands was opened in 1958. The main entrance to the park from Liardet Street is through a grand art deco gateway into the distinctive cricket ground with its grassed viewing platforms cut into the steep hillside (the location for scenes in the film *The Last Samurai*). Beyond the cricket ground, paths lead into the heart of the park, with its fountains, waterfall, tearooms and well-known lake.

The red Poet's Bridge, famous as a foreground for snapshots of the mountain, is not named after any bard, but after a very successful racehorse called The Poet. The bridge was built by the owner with the horse's substantial winnings, and has been restored in recent years. The fabulous fernery, accessed by moss-covered tunnels, was opened in 1928 and now consists of four fern houses dedicated to New Zealand ferns.

The park has renowned azalea and rhododendron gardens, while above the Bowl of Brooklands lies the small Brooklands Zoo and playgrounds (open 9 am to 5 pm, free of charge). Adjacent to the zoo is the historic building The Gables, and nearby are the oriental Kunming Gardens.

The Bowl of Brooklands has hosted many famous artists since the late 1950s, and today is regular host to internationally recognised acts and the popular WOMAD festival (World of Music and Dance).

Not to be missed during the summer months is the TSB Bank Festival of Lights, when the park is lit up with displays of every conceivable type of lights, accompanied by free entertainment.

6 Paritutu Rock Hard 🚶 30 minutes return

* Dramatic coastal views from this old volcanic plug.

➤ Centennial Drive, New Plymouth, near the port.

Paritutu is the remains of an old volcanic plug, and is similar in structure and origin to the small Sugarloaf Islands just offshore. While the climb is steep and not for those afraid of heights, the rocky scramble is made easier by numerous steps and wire railings near the top. The views are spectacular, south along the coast, south-east to the mountain, and north over the port and city. More impressive is that Paritutu is also the site of an old pa. Its strategic and defensive properties are obvious.

7 Koru Pa Easy 🚶 30 minutes return

* An ancient pa site that includes stone work in its construction.

➤ At Oakura turn left into Wairau Road. Follow the signposts 4 km along this road.

Occupied from around AD 1000 to AD 1826, this is one of New Zealand's most ancient pa sites. Overlooking the Oakura River, Koru pa is unusual in the use of stone, which is very rare in New Zealand where wood is much more easily available. The pa site is well preserved with terraces, food pits and defensive ditches all clearly outlined, and extensive use of river stones can be seen on the outer facings of the defensive ditches. The pa is bush-covered which makes exploration more intriguing, though there is a good view of the river from a lookout point. The use of stone is an indication to some theorists that Aotearoa was inhabited by an ancient stone-using culture long before AD 1000.

8 North Egmont

✷ High on the slopes of Mt Taranaki, fascinating alpine vegetation is combined with great views of both the mountain and the province.

➤ 12 km from New Plymouth, turn off SH3 at Egmont Village. Follow Egmont Road to the North Egmont Visitor Centre.

If the summit of Taranaki is too much of a challenge, these four short walks will give visitors a taste of the sub-alpine upper slopes of the mountain. All four walks begin from the North Egmont Visitor Centre, which has excellent displays about the mountain's natural and human history and which also has updated track and weather information. Just behind the Visitor Centre is the historic Camphouse. Originally a military barracks during the Land Wars in the 1860s, it was moved to this site in the 1880s to accommodate the increasing number of visitors to the mountain.

Veronica Loop Track   Medium   🚶 2 hours return

Mt Taranaki has a unique ecosystem as it is isolated from the other mountain areas of the North Island, and also has one of the highest rainfalls in New Zealand. The Veronica Loop Track is entirely within sub-montane forest with lower areas dense with ferns and mosses that flourish in the wet climate, while on the higher slopes of the track the vegetation is more open.

Holly Hut Track Lookout   Medium   🚶 1 hour return

Follow the Veronica Loop Track uphill to the junction with the Holly Hut Track and continue for another 10 minutes along the Holly Hut Track to a lookout with a seat. There are broad views over the Taranaki lowlands, while the mountain looms high above the track. Even within this short distance the vegetation changes markedly from alpine forest to more open sub-alpine shrubs and tussock. While this walk is all uphill, the track is well formed and the grade is more steady than steep.

Ngatoro Loop Walk   Easy   🚶   30 minutes return

Plants thickly cover every surface in this damp goblin forest of alpine beech. Lichens, ferns and mosses in every conceivable shade of green grow over every rock, tree trunk and branch.

Nature Walk   Easy   🚶   15 minutes

This short walk through mountain bush is a good introduction to the Taranaki forest and is suitable for every age and ability.

9 Kapuni Loop Track to Dawson Falls   Medium   🚶   1 hour return

✳ Virgin mountain forest frames an attractive small waterfall on the south side of Mt Taranaki.

➤ From the centre of Stratford, follow the signs to Dawson Falls (19 km).

A long drive through thick bush leads to the Dawson Falls Visitor Centre, which is the start point for a number of tracks on the south flank of Taranaki. The centre has up-to-date information on the tracks and weather, and detailed displays on the unique flora and fauna of this mountain. The falls were rediscovered in 1883 and named after the local postmaster at Manaia, Thomas Dawson, though they were already known to Maori as Te Rere O Noke. The Dawson Falls Hotel was built in 1895 and today still offers accommodation.

The track leading to Dawson Falls is signposted just below the visitors' car park. Leading through moss- and fern-encrusted forest, the track goes down steep steps which can be slippery because of the constant wetness. The 18-metre falls drop over an ancient lava flow throwing up a continuous spray, adding to the normally high rainfall that keeps the vegetation wet throughout the year.

A viewing platform by the car park gives an excellent view of the mountain (weather willing), in particular the lower cone known as Fanthams Peak.

Taranaki, Wanganui and Manawatu

10 Lake Rotokare   Easy   🚶 1½ hours return

* A beautiful bush-fringed lake hidden in the Taranaki hills.

➤ Turn into Anderson Road off SH3 just north of Eltham, then left at Rawhitiroa Road and right into Sangster Road.

Very little lowland forest has survived in Taranaki, so this lake located in hill country east of Eltham comes as a surprise. Most of the other lakes in Taranaki are hydro-lakes, but Rotokare is naturally formed and spring-fed. The flat well-formed track skirts the raupo (reed) beds of this fiord-like small lake, which is densely ringed by forest including kahikatea, maire and totara, though the area was milled well into the middle of last century. The lake is popular with boaties and water skiers, though use is seasonally limited and native bird life is surprisingly prolific.

The beginning of the track is not that clearly marked. It lies just beyond the grassed picnic area by the car park.

11 Patea River   Easy   🚶 40 minutes return

* Post-industrial walk along the Patea River.

➤ The track begins at the end of the road that leads along the western side of the Patea River right by the bridge.

An eerie silence reigns over one of New Zealand's most unusual landscapes. In February 2008 fire swept through the ruined freezing works, destroying most of what was left of the old buildings. The rusting railway leads to derelict and decaying wharves, and alongside the river a battered concrete storeroom sprouts grass from the roof while the old piles decay into the tidal sands.

The walk follows the tidal Patea River along sandy bluffs to the pleasant and tidy picnic area near the old breakwaters. This is a popular spot for very brave surfers riding the waves between the concrete breakwaters, which also create a small safe beach just inside the river mouth.

12 Bushy Park   Easy ⅄ 1 hour

* A rare remnant of lowland rain forest including an ancient rata tree.

➤ Turn off SH3 at Kia Iwi north of Wanganui, and follow Rangitatau East Road for 8 km to Bushy Park.

Owned and administered by Forest and Bird, this 90-hectare bush remnant was bequeathed to the society in 1962 by Frank Moore whose family had farmed the area since the 1860s. The heart of Bushy Park is a magnificent Victorian homestead complete with period furniture, and outbuildings including stables and a small museum.

Visitors enter through double automated gates, as the bush is now surrounded by a predator-proof fence built in 2004 in an effort to restore native birdlife to the park. The bush itself contains a network of tracks, all fairly easy to follow, and there are a host of informative labels and panels that make Bushy Park a great place to improve your knowledge of native trees and shrubs. A highlight among the many large trees is an old rata, the largest surviving example of the northern species. Standing at a height of over 40 metres, it is not easy to miss.

There is a small charge to enter the park. Bushy Park offers light meals, accommodation and conference facilities.

13 Lake Virginia   Easy ⅄ 30 minutes around the lake

* A small park-like lake with an Edwardian atmosphere.

➤ Great North Road (SH3), Wanganui.

Lake Virginia is a small picturesque lake on the outskirts of Wanganui, complete with formal gardens, a winter house, statues, fountains and a band rotunda, creating the pleasant atmosphere of an Edwardian country garden. The aquatic birdlife is prolific with both black and white swans, pukeko, ducks and coots, and at night the trees and fountain are illuminated.

14 Whanganui River   Easy   🚶   Up to 1½ hours

✱ An easy stroll along the banks of the Whanganui River.

➤ Begin at the City Bridge at the end of Victoria Avenue, Wanganui.

From the City Bridge, follow the river upstream along Taupo Quay and then into Somme Parade. This passes some fine restored Victorian commercial buildings, harking back to the days when the river was a major highway into the interior and Wanganui was an important port town. Taupo Quay is the home of the *Waimarie*, the lone survivor of a fleet of paddle steamers that worked the river.

At the Dublin Street bridge cross the river and turn right into Kowhai Park, a long stretch of mature trees, a fantasy children's playground and excellent picnic spots along the river. Just before returning to the City Bridge, take a detour up the elevator to the stone tower crowning Durie Hill. The historic elevator, the only public underground elevator in New Zealand, was built in 1919 to give easy access to the then new hilltop suburbs. The 33-metre tower has great views over the city, and on a clear day both Mt Ruapehu and Taranaki are clearly visible. As an alternative way down, take the steps back to the river.

This walk can be extended north by continuing past the Dublin Street bridge and crossing over the river by the railway bridge, or south by continuing along Taupo Quay to the Cobham Bridge.

15 Historic Wanganui City   Easy   🚶   1 hour

✱ Wanganui is noted for its fine Victorian Buildings, now lovingly restored.

➤ The Information Centre at 101 Guyton Street, Wanganui.

In 1930 Wanganui was New Zealand's fifth-largest city, but the lack of a hinterland and the decline of the river as an important access route deep into the heart of the North Island have meant slower progress in more recent years, leaving Wanganui with an outstanding collection of well-preserved Victorian and Edwardian buildings.

Arm yourself with a map from the Information Centre and include the following landmarks on your walk.

- **National Bank**, corner of Victoria Ave and Maria Place. Looking distinctly Victorian with its huge Ionic columns, this building was actually constructed in 1929.

- **The Bell Tower**, Cooks Gardens, St Hill Street. Mounted on the site of the old York Stockade, the 1874 Sheffield fire bell was used to ring the alarm for any fires in the city.

- **Wanganui Opera House**, 10 St Hill Street. Built in 1899, this wooden building was the centre of entertainment in early Wanganui.

- **Post Office Building**, corner Victoria Avenue and Ridgway Street. The Post Office was an important administration building, but in addition Wanganui was once the North Island terminus of the Cook Strait cable and this grand building edifice, built in 1902, is an appropriate reflection of that status.

- **Queens Park**. Originally the site of the pa Pukenamu, this hill was occupied by the Rutland Stockade during the tense years of the Land Wars. Now the cultural heart of Wanganui, the hill is crowned by the Sarjeant Gallery. Built of Oamaru stone and opened in 1919, it was purpose-built as an art gallery and was designed to take maximum advantage of natural light. To one side of the park is the Whanganui Museum, located in a fine 1921 building and housing a superb waka taua (war canoe), and the finest collection of Lindauer paintings in the country. On the city side of the park is the War Memorial Hall, built in 1960 and winner of the New Zealand Institute of Architects Gold Medal.

- **Taupo Quay Buildings**. The area by the river was once the commercial heart of the city and many fine Victorian and Edwardian mercantile buildings survive from this period.

16 Mangaweka Scenic Reserve   Medium   🚶   45 minutes

✳ A stand of virgin bush sits above Mangaweka township, with a lookout point over the Rangitikei River.

➤ Just south of Mangaweka turn off SH1 into Te Kapua Road. The track begins about 1 km along this road. Look for the small 'DOC Walking Track' sign.

The walk starts along a wide grassy track which is an old section of the main trunk railway line. The fragile nature of the papa rock is evident on this section, with small rocks fallen from the crumbling banks littering the track. The track then climbs steeply into the bush, levelling off as it winds its way through huge old rimu and totara trees. On the downhill section there are excellent views over Mangaweka township, the Rangitikei River, and the dramatic papa cliffs so characteristic of the area.

17 Mangaweka Power Station   Easy   人   20 minutes

* The remains of an old power station set alongside the dramatic Rangitikei River.

➤ Just north of Mangaweka turn off SH1 into Ruahine Road. Cross over the river and take the next left into Kawhatau Valley Road. The power station is on the left after 250 metres.

The road from SH1 drops steeply down to the Rangitikei River with its impressive and highly unstable papa cliffs that make road and rail work in this area inherently difficult.

The power station was built in 1913 primarily as a water reservoir. At the time electricity was considered a minor byproduct, but in fact it made Mangaweka one of the earliest towns in New Zealand to have a power supply. Little remains of the tiny power station, and a small building containing historic photographs shelters the site. The location, however, is impressive. Across the river is the towering rail viaduct over the Rangitikei River, and across the road is a short walk up to the weir along the Mangawharariki River. This beautiful small gorge of rocks, scoured and shaped over aeons by water, leads to a concrete weir that is still intact. To the right of the weir is a small brick-lined tunnel. This was the original water intake for the power station. Still visible in the tunnel is a log that jammed there in 1937, and which caused the station to finally close down. Below the weir is a great swimming hole, though it is a bit of a tricky scramble to get down to.

18 Pryce's Rahui Reserve   Easy   人   30 minutes to 1 hour

* Huge trees in a rare patch of lowland bush.

➤ At Rata turn off SH1 into Putorino Road. The reserve is 8 km down this road.

Though less than 10 km off SH1, this magnificent small bush reserve does not attract many visitors and you are very likely to have the place to yourself. Located on an old river terrace of the Rangitikei River, Pryce's Rahui Reserve contains some huge trees including kahikatea, matai, totara and what must be the country's largest kowhai. Standing at over 10 metres, it certainly makes you reconsider that idea of a kowhai as a 'small' tree suitable for a courtyard garden.

There are a number of tracks marked in different colours, none of them particularly long. (The kowhai is on the red track, and a giant matai can be seen on the yellow track.) The red/blue combination will take around 30 minutes, while the yellow track is around 60 minutes. Though a bit overgrown, the reserve is quite small and you can't get lost.

19 Sledge Track, Kahuterawa Valley

Easy   🚶   1 hour return to Argyle Rocks

✳ A rocky stream cascades down a bush-clad valley.

➤ From Palmerston North start heading south towards Shannon, then turn left towards Woodville on SH57, and just past this junction turn immediately right into Kahuterawa Road. Continue down this road to the car park, which is 3.5 km past where the seal ends. The Kahuterawa Reserve is not the beginning of the track.

The recently opened track begins to the left of the historic Black Bridge, built in 1900, and continues up the left-hand side of the stream along a steep bush-clad valley. The bush is largely regenerating vegetation, but is attractive. Along the track water drips over moss-covered rocks while, below, the stream tumbles over worn river boulders. On the way there are a number of good swimming holes, including Argyle Rocks, a collection of large river boulders creating a pool in the river. Just beyond Argyle Rocks, Foulds Falls is a pretty waterfall on a side stream to the left of the track. The pine plantations on the other side of the valley detract a little from the experience. For the active the track continues on for another 2 km to a lookout point; return by the same track.

20 Victoria Esplanade   Easy   🏃   1 hour

* ✳ Formal gardens, sports fields, and bush walks make this a very popular recreational spot.

* ➤ Fitzherbert Avenue near the Manawatu River in Palmerston North.

Stretching along the banks of the Manawatu River, Victoria Esplanade (as it is known today) took shape under the guidance of Peter Black, the curator of Palmerston North's parks between 1908 and 1946. During this period the formal gardens, arboretum and tropical conservatory were established, and the avenues of cherry trees and phoenix palms were planted. In later years a children's playground, aviary, miniature railway and the old post office, known as Victoria House, were added to the park. Alongside the river five hectares of surviving native bush, one of the largest such remnants in the Manawatu, is laced with easy walking tracks.

21 Savage Crescent   Easy   🏃   1 hour

* ✳ One of the best examples of unaltered early state housing.

* ➤ Access off either College Street or Park Road between Botanical Road and Cook Street in Palmerston North.

One of the key promises of Labour leader Michael Joseph Savage was to provide good housing for New Zealand's working population (as opposed to the poor), and the election of his government in 1935 heralded a boom in state housing that lasted for decades. While state housing is ubiquitous in every New Zealand city and town, what makes Savage Crescent unique is that it is an early example of state domestic architecture, and it has survived largely intact and unaltered. Developed between 1939 and 1946, the housing styles are remarkable and varied, and contrast greatly with the more familiar wooden and tile houses of the 1950s. A park was developed in the heart of the crescent to provide a recreation area for the neighbourhood.

22 Wreck of the *Hyderabad* Easy 人 30 minutes return

✳ High on a beach is the remains of an old sailing ship, the *Hyderabad.*

➤ Off SH1 down Waitarere Beach Road, 6.5 km north of Levin. At the beach turn left into Rua Avenue to Hyderabad Place.

Nothing quite beats the romance of a shipwreck, particularly the wreck of an old sailing ship. The remains of the *Hyderabad* are the rusting outlines of a cotton trader driven hard ashore here in a storm in 1878 on a voyage from Lyttelton to Adelaide. No lives were lost, but the *Hyderabad* could not be refloated. Though its cargo was quickly salvaged, the ship over the years has been stripped of anything valuable. Today only an outline of its ghostly shape still remains, periodically covered and uncovered by the wind-driven sands.

From Hyderabad Place go on to the driftwood-littered beach and walk south for about 10 to 15 minutes. The outline of the wreck is more clearly visible from a distance.

23 Lake Papaitonga Easy 人 40 minutes return to the Otomuri Lookout

✳ Dense virgin bush surrounds a small lake with two historic pa sites.

➤ 4 km south of Levin turn off SH1 into Hokio Beach Road. Lake Papaitonga is signposted to the left.

This little-known gem is a small lake surrounded by the finest lowland bush remnant between Wanganui and Wellington, dominated by titoki, kahikatea, nikau, karaka and kiekie. The lake was the scene of a bloody massacre of the local Muaupoko iwi by the invading Te Rauparaha, despite the protection of their pa on islands in the lake. (The smaller of the two islands was artificially constructed by the Muaupoko iwi in the shallow lake water.) Later the land was acquired by the noted naturalist Sir Walter Butler, and it was Butler who recognised its value and preserved this small piece of bush for future generations.

The track is in excellent condition with boardwalks through the swampy sections and two lookout points over the lakes.

Taranaki, Wanganui and Manawatu

24 Nikau Reserve   Medium 𝕏 45 minutes return

* Dense nikau and kohekohe groves give this reserve a distinctly tropical feel with views out over Cook Strait.

➤ SH1 north of Paraparaumu, opposite the entrance to Lindale Farm.

Despite its SH1 location and smart entrance, this track is poorly maintained, which is a real shame as this is a particularly fine stand of coastal forest. Sunlight filtering through the fronds of the nikau palms and the pale green leaves of the kohekohe trees give this bush a beautiful open light.

The track begins from the 'Nikau Reserve' sign. After a steady uphill climb on a track that is often rough and muddy with fallen branches, a clearing by farmland is reached that has a wonderful view over the coast and beyond to Kapiti Island and the Marlborough Sounds. The return track is quite tricky to find, and many other visitors have made all sorts of false starts, which makes it even more confusing. However, the return track is just to the left where you emerge from the bush into the clearing, and can be recognised by a small bridge immediately on entering the bush. The track returns to the car park.

25 Waikanae River Estuary and Beach
Easy 𝕏 50 minutes return

* The picturesque Waikanae River gives way to views of Kapiti Island along the beach.

➤ Off SH1 at Otaihanga Road (the same access road as the Southward Car Museum). Otaihanga Road leads to Makora Road and the beginning of the walk at the Otaihanga Domain.

This unmarked walk begins over the swing bridge at the Otaihanga Domain, a popular family swimming spot in the clear stony waters of the Waikanae River during the summer months. Turning left, the clear waters quickly give way to the tidal salt marsh of the small estuary, prolific with aquatic and wading birds despite the close proximity of housing. Eventually the track leads to a car park and from there it is a short walk to the beach. With Kapiti Island just 5 km offshore, the area between the beach and the island is now the Kapiti Marine Reserve.

The track is also used by cyclists who are not always considerate of walkers.

26 Queen Elizabeth II Park   Easy   ⅄   1¼ hours

✳ A dune walk with views of Kapiti Island and good swimming.

➤ MacKays Crossing off SH1, just north of Paekakariki.

Queen Elizabeth II Park protects a large area of coastal dunes, wetlands and farmland between Paekakariki and Raumati. It can be accessed at several points, though the most popular entrance is at MacKays Crossing by the Wellington Tramway Museum. The central car park at Whareroa Beach is the start point for two loop walks, one north towards Raumati and the other south towards Paekakariki. Both walks have a seaward track that follows the dunes with many excellent viewpoints over the beach out to Kapiti Island and south to Mana Island, and across Cook Strait the rugged hills of the Marlborough Sounds are clearly visible. Looping back on the inland track through farm and wetland, the going is more sheltered from the prevailing westerlies. Depending on the tide and wind, another option is to walk part of the way along the beach. Both loop walks will take around 1¼ hours. Swimming on this section of coast is generally very safe.

The historic tram runs from the main road to the beach on the weekend, so you can park by the museum and catch the tram to the beach – a popular option especially if you have children.

Taranaki, Wanganui and Manawatu

Wellington and Wairarapa

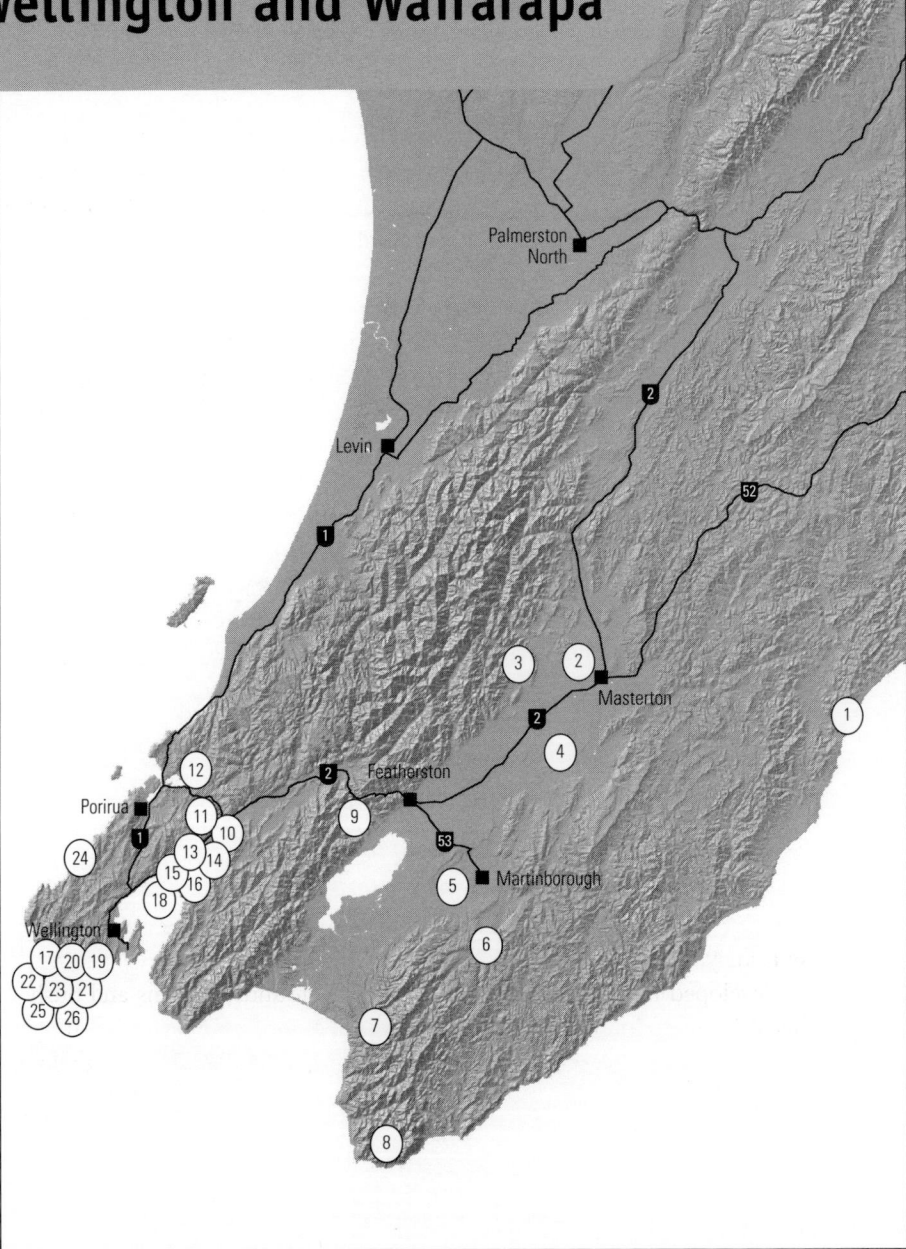

1 Castle Point   Easy 🚶 40 minutes

✳ A classic lighthouse sits high above some of the most stunning coastal scenery in the country.

➤ Some 65 km north-east of Masterton.

Known for safe swimming, surf and fishing, the setting of Castle Point is dramatic, with the lighthouse atop the raw cliff face of Castle Point and overlooking the coastal settlement. The lighthouse is one of New Zealand's most stylish, with a slender taper from 5 metres at its base to 3 metres at the top. Built in 1912, the lighthouse could be seen 30 km out to sea, and was only automated in 1988.

The wild coast here is spectacular. Huge waves, directly off the Southern Ocean, hammer the cliffs below the lighthouse, and thunder and crash over the rocky reef that protects the lagoon.

The walk initially crosses the sandy spit between the surf beach and the lagoon on a raised boardwalk, and gradually climbs up to the lighthouse. From the lighthouse the track drops down to a lookout point, and it is possible to clamber around the rocks back to a point just above the boardwalk. Take some time to climb up the rocks overlooking the reef and lagoon, a very popular spot for fishing. However, take very good care in this area as one false step or rogue wave and you're a goner …

2 Lake Henley   Easy 🚶 Up to 1 hour

✳ A pleasant walk around a lake in a park ideal for all the family.

➤ On Te Ore Ore Road off SH2, 2 km north of Masterton.

Lake Henley was formed from an old bend in the Ruamahanga River and has been developed into a delightful park with playgrounds, gardens and bush walks. A walk around the small lake will take about 20 minutes with further walks extending down to the river that take longer. The lake is a haven for ducks, pukeko and a wide range of aquatic wildlife.

/

Wellington and Wairarapa

3 Mt Holdsworth

✳ Beautiful rugged bush lines a very attractive valley stream in the foothills of the Tararua Range.

➤ From Masterton take SH2 to 1 km south of the Waingawa River bridge. Turn right into Norfolk Road and travel a further 16 km to the parking area.

Tucked in the foothills of the Tararua Range alongside the Atiwhakatu Stream, Holdsworth is the starting point for numerous walks ranging from 5 minutes to 5 hours. For the casual visitor this is one of the more accessible points in the Tararuas. The following two walks start just over the swing bridge, about 5 minutes' walk from the car park. The camping area, set in a glade by the river, is particularly attractive.

Mt Holdsworth Lookout   Hard 🚶 1¼ hours return

This solid uphill trudge is not actually up Mt Holdsworth, but instead leads to a lookout point with a view of Mt Holdsworth deep in the Tararua Range across the valley. Beech is the predominate tree, but keep an eye out for the very rare native mistletoe protected in wire cages from browsing possums. About halfway up is the remains of a pa punanga, which acted as a refuge for non-combatants deep in the bush during times of trouble.

The track begins to the left just over the swing bridge.

Donnelly's Flat Loop Track   Easy 🚶 1 hour return

A flat walk through magnificent beech and rimu to a clearing on the Atiwhakatu Stream, a clear rocky stream in a bush-clad valley. Gold was discovered in this area in 1873, though it never was found in any quantity, and the flat is named after Tom Donnelly, a goldminer who died from injuries on Mt Holdsworth. The clearing is a wide grassy area with access to the river complete with barbecues and picnic tables. Beyond the flat, the walk swings away from the river and passes through a huge swathe of delicate kidney fern that covers both sides of the track. These ferns appear very fragile, and in the hot dry Wairarapa summer shrivel to the texture of old crumpled paper in order to conserve moisture until the next rain.

The loop track starts to the right over the swing bridge.

4 Carter Scenic Reserve   Easy 🚶 20 minutes

* The largest bush remnant on the Wairarapa Plain.

➤ From SH2 in Carterton take Park Road towards Gladstone (signposted from the Carterton shopping centre). From Park Road turn left into Carters Line and then right into Gladstone Road and, after 3 km, the reserve is on the right.

This 31-hectare reserve was bequeathed by Charles Carter, an early Wairarapa pioneer (after whom the nearby town Carterton is named). Sitting alongside the Ruamahanga River, the reserve is low-lying and swampy, with kahikatea, flax and other water-loving plants dominating the vegetation. Boardwalks cross the wettest parts. In many respects the reserve has a rather battered and forlorn appearance, leading one to be rather sad that this is all that is left of the lowland forest.

5 Rapaki Hillside Walk   Easy 🚶 1 hour return

* An open farmland track with surprising bucolic views of the Wairarapa.

➤ From Martinborough head west on Jellicoe Street towards Lake Ferry. The walk is signposted to the left, 2 km from town.

Located on private land through the kindness of the local farm owners, this track leads gently uphill to a surprising broad view of the Wairarapa. Below is Martinborough, surrounded by vineyards, and beyond to the east is the forested Aorangi Range. North and west are the flat plains, bisected by the Ruamahanga River and bordered by Lake Ferry and the Tararua Range. This a particularly pleasant walk on a warm summer's evening.

6 Ruakokopatuna Caves   Easy 🚶 40 minutes

* A rocky steam runs though a cave with glow-worms.

➤ Take Jellicoe Street from Martinborough for 6 km, then turn left into Dry River Road. After 9 km turn into Blue Rock Road. The caves are 3 km down this unsealed road.

This cave, located on private land, follows an underground stream through limestone rock and has a sprinkling of glow-worms. The track is unformed, you will get your feet wet, a torch is handy, and donations are appreciated. This is a good first cave experience for the very young.

7 Putangirua Pinnacles   Easy   🏃 1½ hours return

* ✳ Spectacular pinnacles formed by erosion.

* ➤ 12 km south on the Cape Palliser Road from the junction with Lake Ferry Road. The walk starts by the picnic area and camping ground.

Over many thousands of years the Putangirua Stream has eroded the soft coastal soils to create an unusual 'badlands' landscape of deep gullies and tall pillar-like formations known as 'hoodoos'. Hoodoos are formed when rock protects the soil from rain and prevents the soft gravels from eroding, creating high fluted formations. While quite common along the coast, at Putangirua the concentration of hoodoos in one small valley is spectacular, made even more so by the fact that the walk takes you right into the heart of the valley.

The track follows the riverbed up from the picnic area and camping ground at the entrance to the walk. As the river is subject to frequent seasonal flooding there is no official track as such; just follow the riverbed up to the wide valley that leads off to the left. The riverbed is rocky and uneven so good footwear is recommended.

8 Cape Palliser Lighthouse   Medium   🏃 20 minutes return

* ✳ A picture-perfect lighthouse sitting high above the wild scenery of the southern Wairarapa coast.

* ➤ From Martinborough take the road south towards Lake Ferry, then turn to the left onto the road to Ngawi. The lighthouse is 5 km past Ngawi.

Nearly 260 steps lead to this historic lighthouse painted in red and white horizontal stripes in the most traditional manner. Located 78 metres above the sea, the 18-metre tall lighthouse was built in 1897 to guide shipping around the perilous Cape Palliser, a coastline that combines rocky headlands and shoals with fierce weather blasting straight up from the Southern Ocean.

From the lighthouse keeper's cottage the steps lead straight up the rocky bluff to fantastic views along the coast. Succulents and coprosma thrive in crevices of the raw hillside.

About halfway between Ngawi and the lighthouse keep an eye out for the seal colony on the rocks below. Take care if you plan to have a closer look, as many seals rest right beside the road and are not easy to spot until you are almost on top of them. They can be aggressive.

The road to Ngawi is excellent. Sealed, mainly straight, it follows the coast with just one or two rough patches through the unstable terrain. The last section from Ngawi is unsealed.

9 Rimutaka Trig Medium 𝄎 45 minutes return

* Excellent views over the Tararua Range and the Wairarapa plain.

➤ The track begins just below the west side of the Rimutaka Summit on SH2, where the sign says 'Welcome To Upper Hutt'.

Make no mistake about it, the Rimutaka Trig is definitely sub-alpine both in vegetation and in climate. Even on a fine day it blows up here, and in very windy conditions think twice about climbing this track. If it is cloudy just don't bother: you won't see a thing. On good day, however, make the effort; it is a steady rather than steep climb and the views from the 725-metre trig point over the Wairarapa, Rimutaka Range and Lake Ferry are worth it. If the wind on the summit gets a bit much, grab a respite in the tiny hollow just below the top, which with a bit of shelter supports large shrubs and acts as a very effective wind-break.

10 Kaitoke Regional Park Easy 𝄎 1 hour

* Beautiful untouched forest lines the Hutt River as it cuts through the foothills of the Tararua Range.

➤ The park is clearly signposted at Waterworks Road off SH2, 12 km north of Upper Hutt. The walks described begin from Pakuratahi, 1 km on from the main information board and ranger office.

In 1939 large areas of virgin bush were purchased for the local water supply catchment area. Today half of Wellington's water is still drawn from the Hutt River from within the park. Now covering 2860 hectares, the park has some of the finest untouched bush in the Wellington region, with magnificent stands of old rimu, rata and beech.

There are a number of walks from Pukuratahi, which can easily be combined as some are very short. The main walk, a loop along the Hutt River, begins over a long swing bridge from the car park. Immediately over the bridge is a short nature walk with interpretive panels that will take around 15 minutes to complete. The main track continues through magnificent forest to the Flume Bridge, from which there are views down the Hutt River gorge. Over the bridge is the Kaitoke Strainer House, which acted as an initial filter for the water system. Located on the wall of the house is a fascinating map of Wellington's impressive water system which is well worth a good look. From here the track follows the sealed access road back to the car park; instead of walking along the road, take the short Terrace Track which runs parallel to the road and has very fine bush with excellent tree identification signs.

Near the car park a short side path leads to the site of Rivendell from the Lord of the Rings films. Although nothing now remains, a helpful panel shows stills from the film of the river setting below.

In addition to the walks, there are great picnic sites and swimming holes in the river.

11 Tunnel Gully, Tane's Track   Easy   ⅄   1 hour

✳ An historic railway tunnel and magnificent beech forest.

➤ Turn right into Plateau Road off SH2 at the Te Marua store just north of Upper Hutt.

It is easier to do the Tane's Track loop walk anticlockwise as the signage in the first part of the track is a bit unclear, though you won't get lost. Begin from the car park. The track leads to the right, and it takes about 5 minutes to reach the tunnel. The Mangaroa Tunnel was built in 1875 and is lined with a curious and inconsistent mixture of brick and stone. At just over 220 metres long, a torch is helpful but not essential. After exploring the tunnel return to the large grassed area; walk diagonally across this area, past the mountain-bike track to the right, and on to Tane's Track. At this point the track enters the bush and loops through some stunning beech forest with enormous trees hundreds of years old. Near the end of the walk near the car park is an immensely tall rimu. Along the way there is also a small picturesque waterfall trickling down mossy rocks.

If you just want to go to the tunnel a loop walk will take around 20 minutes. The track and facilities are very well maintained.

12 Pauatahanui Wildlife Reserve Easy 🚶 20 minutes to 1 hour

✱ A vast tidal marsh complete with bird hides is home to numerous wading birds.

➤ Off SH58 at Pauatahanui, between Paremata and Haywards in the Hutt Valley.

The largest unmodified estuarine salt marsh in the southern half of the North Island, the Pauatahanui Wildlife Reserve is a haven for wading and migratory birds. Five hides, all within easy walking distance, provide plenty of opportunity for keen birdwatchers to observe the wildlife. The casual visitor will enjoy the quiet of the salt marsh and the subtle shades of estuary vegetation ranging from every shade of green through to the brown, yellow and red of the tidal grasses.

Since 1984 the local Forest and Bird branch has worked not only to restore the wetland environment but also to provide excellent access with paths, boardwalks and information boards.

13 Belmont Trig Hard 🚶 2 hours return

✱ Wide views that take in the whole Wellington area and out over the Cook Strait to the South Island.

➤ Follow Dowse Drive up from the Western Hutt motorway just north of the Petone turn-off. Turn left into Stratton Street and follow the signs to the car park on the right. The track starts just down the hill from the car park.

The huge sprawling Belmont Regional Park spreads between the Hutt Valley and the Porirua basin. While mainly farmland and gorse with the occasional valley of regenerating scrub, the park was only established in 1981 and future generations will benefit from the foresight of setting aside this vast area for a park. The track to the Belmont Trig is a solid uphill slog through farmland on a wide 4WD track that is a steady grade, but the views are worth it. At 457 metres, the trig point is the highest point in the park and the views from here are endless, over Porirua, Hutt Valley, Wellington Harbour and city, and far across Cook Strait to the Marlborough Sounds and the Kaikoura Mountains. In the distance are the Rimutaka, Orongorongo and Tararua Ranges. What is even better is that the view is not revealed until the very top.

Just below the summit is a small patch of bush that is worth exploring. While the trees are battered by the constant wind, the understorey is luxuriant with delicate ferns and tender mosses.

Wellington and Wairarapa

14 Korokoro Dam Medium ⚐ 50 minutes

✳ A track leads down through a deep sheltered gully to the old Petone water reservoir.

➤ Follow Dowse Drive up from the Western Hutt motorway just north of the Petone turn-off. From Dowse Drive follow the signs to the Oakleigh Street car park.

Built in 1903 to supply the Petone borough with water, Korokoro was the first gravity-fed concrete dam in New Zealand. It is still an attractive multi-tiered dam, set in lush bush which has been protected since the dam was built and contains mature nikau, rimu, rata, tawa and kohekohe. The name Korokoro is closely related to the Maori name for the North Island, Te Ika A Maui or the Great Fish of Maui. In Maori legend the whole island is the fish, Wellington Harbour is the mouth, and the Korokoro Valley is the throat.

The loop track begins to the left of the information board, and drops steeply down to the Korokoro Stream. The return walk is longer and a much gentler grade.

15 Hutt River Trail Easy

✳ An easy walk along the picturesque Hutt River.

➤ Ewen Bridge in the Lower Hutt City Centre.

⚐ Ewen Bridge to Ava Bridge: 40 minutes return

Ewen Bridge to Melling Bridge: 40 minutes return

Running nearly 30 km from the Hikoikoi Reserve in Petone to Birchville in Upper Hutt, this flat trail is a dream for cycling, walking and running, as well as giving great access to the Hutt River for kayaking, swimming and fishing (there are good trout to be had in this river).

Two loop walks begin from the Ewen Bridge. They cover both sides of the river, one going north to the Melling Bridge and the other going south to the Ava Bridge. Both walks follow the stopbanks on the eastern side that protect Lower Hutt and Petone from flooding. It was the constant flooding that forced the early settlers to abandon Petone and re-establish the colony in Port Nicholson on the other side of the harbour.

16 Butterfly Creek   Medium

✴ Beech forest surrounds a popular swimming and picnic spot in a deep valley behind Eastbourne.

➤ The two most common entry points are Kowhai Street and Muritai Park in Eastbourne.

🚶 From Kowhai Street: 1½ hours

From Muritai Park: 2 hours

Butterfly Creek runs parallel to the coast, and is isolated by a steep low ridge that shelters the valley from the worst of both the southerly and northerly winds. This deep valley of rata, beech and rimu forest is a very popular walking spot, and the track following the valley has several entry points from Eastbourne. All involve a steady uphill climb over the ridge, but the uphill walk is compensated for by views over the harbour, Matiu/Somes Island, Wellington city and the Hutt Valley.

The track is in excellent condition and leads to an attractive picnic spot in a glade of beech trees and a small swimming hole in the creek. Kowhai Street and Muritai Park are only 1 km apart, so it is possible to create a loop walk that will take a little over 2 hours to complete.

17 Wellington Botanic Garden   Medium 🚶 1 hour

✴ A combination of formal and wild elements in this historic garden.

➤ The main entrance is on Tinakori Road, Thorndon. The top entrance is from the cable car.

Planting in the Wellington Botanic Garden (established 1844) began in 1868 and today the garden is both a Garden of National Significance and classified as an historic area by the New Zealand Historic Places Trust. The hilly terrain has led to a unique public garden that combines formal plantings with bushy valleys interlinked by winding paths and hidden dells.

The formal garden, at the Tinakori Road entrance, is famous for its spectacular spring display of tulips. It has a sound-shell which hosts small concerts in summer. A short uphill walk from the main entrance leads to the formal beds of the Lady Norwood Rose garden, opened in 1953 and named after the wife of Wellington Mayor Sir Charles Norwood. It contains over

Wellington and
Wairarapa

100 formal rose beds, each bed with a different cultivar. The Begonia House, in addition to the usual collection of tropical and flowering plants, features the giant water lily *Victoria amazonica*, best seen in the summer months. The Visitor Centre is located in the middle of the garden, in the appropriately named Tree House, below which are the garden's older buildings including the original stables.

The paths through the garden are not straightforward. A popular access point is from the cable car, which makes most of the walking downhill. Take time out to visit the fascinating old Bolton Street Cemetery which is accessed off the rose gardens.

18 Matiu/Somes Island   Easy 人 2 hours

* This island combines fascinating human history with an important nature sanctuary.

➤ East by West stops at the island on its cross-harbour ferry route. See www.eastbywest.co.nz or phone 04 499 1282.

Located in the heart of Wellington Harbour, this 25-hectare island has a long history of human occupation and is now an important nature sanctuary free from predators. The legendary explorer Kupe discovered the harbour around AD 1000 and named the island Matiu after a female relative. Maori did occupy the island, but it lacked permanent fresh water and was mainly used as a refuge. Purchased by the New Zealand Company and renamed Somes after the deputy governor of the Company, Joseph Somes, the island was used as a quarantine station from 1872 for both people and animals. During both world wars the island was a detention centre for alien residents. In the First World War detainees included, in addition to Germans, a Turk, a Dutchman, a Swiss and a Mexican. During the Second World War members of Wellington's Italian, German and Austrian community were detained on the island, even though many were in fact refugees. Most of today's buildings are from the animal quarantine period, though the barracks (1890) and a hospital (1915) still remain. There are the remains of anti-aircraft gun emplacements from the Second World War, though the guns were never fired and have long since been removed.

Now the island is an important wildlife sanctuary, and thanks to extensive replanting by the local Forest and Bird branch a surprising proportion of the island now has bush cover. Rare kakariki (New Zealand parakeets) are common on the island. Like blackbirds they forage in the leaf litter on the forest floor and swoop and chatter overhead. It is clear from their lack of shyness and ground-feeding habits why they are so vulnerable to predators and have become nearly extinct on the mainland.

On arriving on the island a good option is to head uphill to the Visitor Centre and spend a few minutes bringing yourself up to date with the island's history. From there head further uphill to the gun emplacements, which not only have a great view over the harbour but give a clear outline of the island. From that point you can access the island circuit track, which is well formed, easy walking and for the most part high up on the island with excellent views all the way around.

19 Mount Victoria   Medium   🚶 1 hour return

* ✳ Great views over the city, the harbour and Hutt Valley, and south to Lyall Bay, Evans Bay and the airport.

* ➤ The track begins in Charles Plimmer Park, off Hawker Street, Mount Victoria.

The most accessible of Wellington's numerous hills, Mount Victoria rises 196 metres above Evans Bay to the east and Port Nicholson to the west, and has fantastic views over the city, Cook Strait, Hutt Valley and the Tararua Range. The strange pyramid-type monument is dedicated to American explorer Rear Admiral Richard Evelyn Byrd, an ardent supporter of the Antarctic Treaty protecting 'the white continent of peace'.

The peak is known to Maori as Tangi Te Keo. Legend has it that when the taniwha Whataitai died, his soul transformed itself into a bird, Te Keo, and flew to this point to mourn the taniwha's death.

There is a maze of tracks up and down the city flank of Mount Victoria, and the signage is neither clear nor consistent. However, you can't get too lost by applying this simple rule: walk uphill on the way there, and downhill on the way back.

✻ The old wharf area is packed with art, museums, adventure activities, restaurants and history.

➤ Can be started at any point, but the walk is described from Oriental Bay to the Railway Station.

Wellington's waterfront is fabulous. Successive city councils and a vigilant, and rightly protective, public have ensured that this area is one of New Zealand's best public spaces, if not in fact the best. No visit to Wellington can be complete without a stroll along the seafront. It is alive with activity from joggers and kayakers through to ferry commuters and restaurant goers, packed with history, and thronged by visitors to museums, art galleries and theatres.

Highlights, in order from Oriental Bay, include:

• Oriental Bay, a pleasant, sandy inner-city beach named after a 19th-century immigrant ship, centred on a fine old band rotunda and lined with stately Norfolk pines.

• The old ferryboat *Tapuhi II*, now a floating restaurant.

• The Freyberg indoor swimming pool.

• Blue and white boatsheds lining the small marina of pleasure craft at Clyde Quay.

• Waitangi Park with its innovative water gardens and playing fields.

• The yacht *Rona*, built in 1893 and looking as modern as the day she was launched.

• Museum of New Zealand, Te Papa Tongarewa, looming large and grey, and packed full of national treasures and art.

• *Hikutaia*, a steam-powered floating crane built in 1926.

• The dramatic statue of Kupe, discoverer of Aotearoa.

• The old boatsheds, overlooking a small lagoon and home to Wellington rowers.

• Paratene Matchitt's City to Sea Bridge, a fantasy link to the Civic Square, the old and new Town Halls, Wellington Art Galley and the Wellington Public Library designed by architect Ian Athfield.

• Frank Kitts Park, a children's playground centred on a lighthouse.

- The Museum of Wellington City & Sea, located in the old Bond Store (built 1892).
- The New Zealand Academy of Fine Arts, established in 1892 and dedicated to exhibiting the best of New Zealand art.
- Shed 5 and Shed 3, built in 1887 and the oldest buildings on the waterfront; now restaurants.
- Wellington Railway Station, built in 1937 in the Beaux Arts style.

21 Wellington by Night   Easy 🏃 Walking time 1 hour, but allow for 5 hours

✳ New Zealand's most lively downtown caters for everyone from 18 to 80.

➤ Begin at Thistle Inn on the corner of Mulgrave Street and Kate Sheppard Place.

Nowhere else in New Zealand quite matches Wellington for lively and varied nightlife suiting just about every taste. Smart restaurants sit side by side with Irish pubs and noodle houses, contemporary theatre mingles with strip clubs, the opera house is next to a gaming parlour, and indie films are on offer along with modern blockbusters.

Start at the northern end of the city, as this quarter tends to be at its most lively after work and in the early evening. At the historic Thistle Inn, built in 1840, the warm wooden interior is lined with historic maps and photos and a glass section in the floor gives a peek into an ancient beer cellar. Around the corner in Molesworth Street, opposite Parliament, is the Backbencher, famous for its grotesque caricatures of New Zealand political figures. You might even spot the odd MP or political journalist in the flesh.

From there continue on to the two pubs on the corner of Featherston and Johnston Streets, where the Three Feathers and the Leuven cater for English and Belgian tastes. From here you can divert to the waterfront to the smart restaurants in Wellington's oldest wharf buildings, Shed 5 and Shed 3.

Continue along the waterfront to Mac's Brewery in Shed 22 near Te Papa and next to Wellington's lively Circa Theatre, established in 1976 and still going strong. Continue to number 16 Taranaki Street to one of Wellington's iconic eating establishments, the Green Parrot. Opened in 1926 by jumped seaman Mr Eddie, the Green Parrot is famous for its hearty meals under a succession of mainly Greek owners cooking on its famous grill made out of reshaped gun barrels.

Just up from the Green Parrot is the long-established Irish pub Molly Malones, formerly the Clarendon Hotel. Turn right into Manners Street and on the right is Wellington's historic State Opera House, built in 1914 and very little altered since that time. From here turn left into Cuba Street, Wellington's most diverse street.

Despite years of change Cuba Street still retains its off-beat atmosphere and in essence is little altered from the early 20th century when it was home to opium dens and (in the 1960s) Carmen's Coffee House, run by Wellington's most famous transvestite. Adult bookshops, smart bars, cheap Asian restaurants, raucous Irish pubs, elegant restaurants and hip cafés make happy neighbours in this shabby chic district.

Finally, head back to Courtenay Place, once a down-at-heel business area, and now alive virtually 24 hours a day. Wellington's oldest picture theatre, the Paramount, shows independent movies while down the road is a huge 10-theatre multiplex. Side streets house very chic bars and nightclubs, and this area has two live theatres, Downstage and Bats, as well as the grand renovated St James Theatre which hosts large shows and concerts. At the end of Courtenay Place is the Embassy Theatre which held the world premier of the third Lord of the Rings film. In amongst all this are restaurants of every description – and check out the Welsh Dragon Bar located in the old men's toilet in middle of Kent Terrace.

22 Zealandia: The Karori Wildlife Sanctuary
Easy   🚶   1½ hours

✳ Some of New Zealand's rarest birds and animals are located in this bush reserve in the heart of Wellington.

➤ Waiapu Road, Karori (www.visitzealandia.com, phone 04 920 9200).

Only 2 km from the city, this 250-hectare forest was originally Wellington city's water reservoir catchment area and was closed to the public for over 120 years. In the early 1990s Forest and Bird members developed a plan to create an urban sanctuary for native flora and fauna, and from this emerged a charitable trust, the Karori Wildlife Sanctuary.

A key to the success of the sanctuary was the erection of 8.6 km of predator-proof fencing (a world first), followed by the eradication of predators within the fenced area. Only recently opened to the public, the park has been a resounding success and is now home to numerous native birds including saddleback, weka, brown teal, tomtit, kaka, whitehead and kiwi, as well as New Zealand's unique native reptile, the tuatara (best seen on a summer afternoon). The tracks and trails are easily accessible and suitable for all levels of fitness. You can even take a boat trip on the lower lake. For an additional fee, experienced guides lead 2-hour tours, and for something different a night tour is also available. Evening hours are extended in summer, making the reserve accessible in the early evening when the birds are more active.

The reserve is open daily from 10 am to 5 pm (last entry 4 pm), longer in the summer. There is an entry fee.

23 Otari–Wilton's Bush Native Botanic Garden and Forest Reserve   Easy 人 1 hour

✸ An outstanding collection of New Zealand flora in a bush reserve.

➤ Wilton Road, Wilton.

A 'must' for anyone interested in New Zealand plants, these gardens are dedicated exclusively to native plants. Pioneer botanist Dr Leonard Cockayne, who was instrumental in collecting and classifying many native plants, established the gardens in 1926 as the Otari Open-Air Plant Museum.

The gardens are beautifully laid out and easily accessible, with the dramatic Canopy Walkway linking the two cultivated parts of the gardens. To the left of the Information Centre are the older gardens with impressive collections of hebe, flax, coprosma and threatened species (among others), while the fernery and alpine gardens in the themed area are equally worth visiting. The Nature Walk loop, which covers both gardens and an attractive section of bush between the two, takes around 40 minutes though it does have a steep section with steps. Beyond the Kaiwharawhara Stream are several loop walks through original bush areas that can take up to 1 hour.

24 Makara Walkway   Hard 🚶 1½ hours return to Fort Opau

✳ Spectacular coastal views over Cook Strait.

➤ From the western end of Karori take Makara Road to the beach.

Exposed to both northerly and southerly winds, the sheer wildness of Makara is its essential appeal. This hasn't always been the case. Several Maori pa sites in the area are testament to the richness of both sea and forest, and James Cook remarked on the din of the dawn chorus of bird song from the coastal forest even though he was almost a kilometre offshore.

The walk begins at the southern end of the beach and traverses farmland as the track climbs solidly uphill, but the views along the way are magnificent, steadily unfolding as you climb. To the right is a ridge that leads to an ancient Ngati Ira pa and higher still is Fort Opau, a Second World War gun emplacement built to protect Cook Strait. The strategic value of the site to both Maori and Pakeha is immediately obvious. The whole of Cook Strait is in clear view, with Mana and Kapiti Islands to the north, the Marlborough Sounds to the west, and the Kaikoura Mountains to the south. The fort was extensive in its heyday, but now only the lookout posts and the gun emplacements partially dug into the hillside still remain.

If the climb up to the fort does not appeal, a return walk to the pa site takes around 50 minutes return and a flat walk along the coast to the point below the pa about 25 minutes return.

25 Café to Café   Easy 🚶 1½ hours

✳ A wild walk along the southern coast links two character Wellington cafés.

➤ The walk can start from either café, in Lyall Bay or Island Bay.

This walk follows Wellington's dramatic southern coast and links two of the city's popular cafés: the Maranui Surf Club in Lyall Bay and The Bach in Island Bay.

Lyall Bay, facing directly into the Southern Ocean, is one of the area's best surf beaches and there are few days when the surf is not running. It is also a great spot to watch planes take off and land at Wellington's busy airport. From Lyall Bay walk south to the rocky South Headland Reserve, dramatic in wild weather when huge waves thrash this coastline. Continue around to

Houghton Bay, where surf rushes up the shingle beach and small houses hug close to the loose greywacke hillsides, on which only the toughest plants such as coprosma and flax grow. Blue penguins regularly nest under houses along this coast, keeping the inhabitants awake at night with their noisy social behaviour.

From Houghton Bay the road leads to Island Bay, sheltering a small fishing fleet in the lee of its namesake Taputeranga Island. Home to Wellington's Italian and Shetland Island communities, each year Island Bay holds a colourful festival in February to bless the fleet, ensuring safety and prosperity in the year ahead.

26 Red Rocks Easy 🚶 1½ hours

✳ An unusual outcrop of distinctly red-coloured rocks along Wellington's wild southern coast.

➤ At Owhiro Bay, follow Owhiro Bay Parade west to the car park at the end.

There is no need for signage at Red Rocks Point as the striking red pillow lava, formed underwater over 200 million years ago, is obvious. A 4WD track follows the wild exposed coast where bull kelp swirls in the brutal tides and oystercatchers scuttle along the stony beaches. Huge shingle fans, reminiscent of the South Island high country, sweep down the barren cliffs, and offshore the Cook Strait ferries buck in the ocean swells.

The only thing that spoils this scene is the 4WD vehicles, not all of which are considerate to walkers. These are not such a problem during the week when few people are about, or on Sunday when the track is closed to vehicles, but the busy 4WD traffic can be very unpleasant on a Saturday.

Glossary of Maori terms

Aotearoa	Land of the Long White Cloud; New Zealand
hapu	sub-tribe
Hawaiki	legendary Pacific homeland of Maori
iwi	tribe
kumara	Maori sweet potato
kumara pits	storage pits for kumara
marae	meeting area of iwi; central area of village
moa	any of several extinct species of large flightless bird
pa	stockaded village
pa punanga	place of refuge
pou	upright post, sometimes carved
rangatira	chief
taniwha	mythical and usually monstrous water spirit
tapu	sacred; forbidden
tohunga	priest
waka	canoe
whare	house, building

Notes

Notes

Other books by Peter Janssen and New Holland Publishers

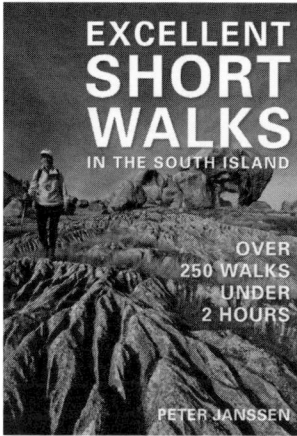

EXCELLENT
SHORT
WALKS
IN THE SOUTH ISLAND

OVER
250 WALKS
UNDER
2 HOURS

PETER JANSSEN

ISBN 978-1-86966-190-8

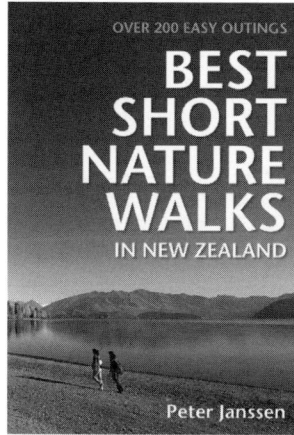

OVER 200 EASY OUTINGS

BEST
SHORT
NATURE
WALKS
IN NEW ZEALAND

Peter Janssen

ISBN 978-1-86966-288-2

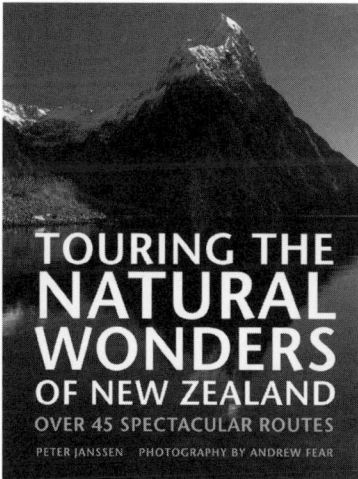

TOURING THE
NATURAL
WONDERS
OF NEW ZEALAND
OVER 45 SPECTACULAR ROUTES

PETER JANSSEN   PHOTOGRAPHY BY ANDREW FEAR

ISBN 978-1-86966-234-9

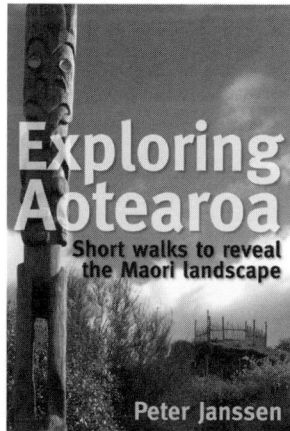

Exploring
Aotearoa
Short walks to reveal
the Maori landscape

Peter Janssen

ISBN 978-1-86966-343-8
Publishing October 2012

Other New Zealand outdoor guides by New Holland Publishers

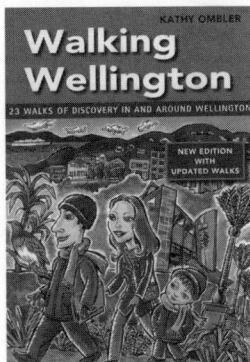

Walking Wellington
KATHY OMBLER
23 WALKS OF DISCOVERY IN AND AROUND WELLINGTON
NEW EDITION WITH UPDATED WALKS
ISBN 978-1-86966-227-1

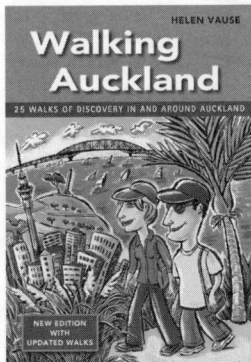

Walking Auckland
HELEN VAUSE
25 WALKS OF DISCOVERY IN AND AROUND AUCKLAND
NEW EDITION WITH UPDATED WALKS
ISBN 978-1-86966-206-6

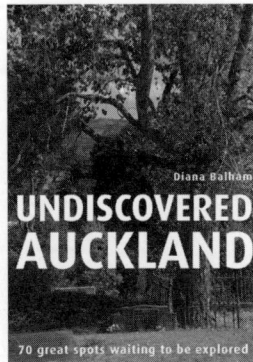

UNDISCOVERED AUCKLAND
Diana Balham
70 great spots waiting to be explored
ISBN 978-1-86966-200-4

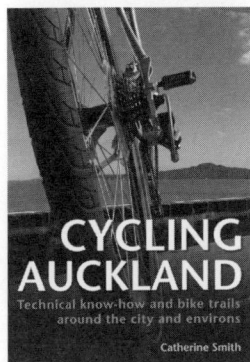

CYCLING AUCKLAND
Technical know-how and bike trails around the city and environs
Catherine Smith
ISBN 978-1-86966-318-6

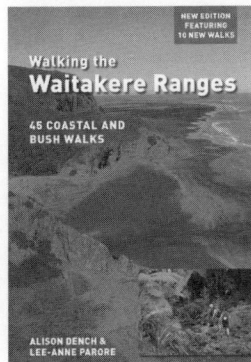

Walking the Waitakere Ranges
NEW EDITION FEATURING 10 NEW WALKS
45 COASTAL AND BUSH WALKS
ALISON DENCH & LEE-ANNE PARORE
ISBN 978-1-86966-218-9

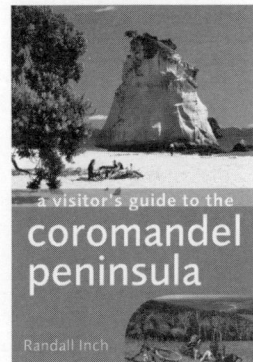

coromandel peninsula
a visitor's guide to the
Randall Inch
ISBN 978-1-86966-164-9

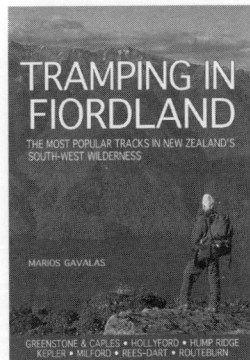

TRAMPING IN FIORDLAND
THE MOST POPULAR TRACKS IN NEW ZEALAND'S SOUTH-WEST WILDERNESS
MARIOS GAVALAS
GREENSTONE & CAPLES • HOLLYFORD • HUMP RIDGE KEPLER • MILFORD • REES-DART • ROUTEBURN
ISBN 978-1-86966-153-3

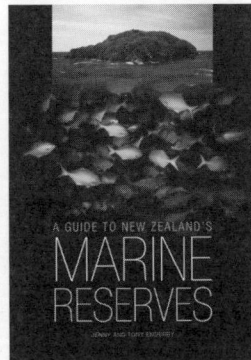

A GUIDE TO NEW ZEALAND'S MARINE RESERVES
JENNY AND TONY ENDERBY
ISBN 978-1-86966-114-4

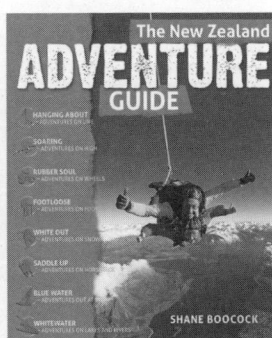

The New Zealand ADVENTURE GUIDE
HANGING ABOUT – ADVENTURES ON HIGH
SOARING – ADVENTURES ON HIGH
RUBBER SOUL – ADVENTURES ON WHEELS
FOOTLOOSE – ADVENTURES ON FOOT
WHITE OUT – ADVENTURES ON SNOW
SADDLE UP – ADVENTURES ON HORSE
BLUE WATER – ADVENTURES OUT AT SEA
WHITEWATER – ADVENTURES ON LAKES AND RIVERS
SHANE BOOCOCK
ISBN 978-1-86966-277-6